Gifted Children and the Law: Mediation, Due Process, and Court Cases

Frances A. Karnes, Ph.D.
and
Ronald G. Marquardt, Ph.D., J.D.

Published by Ohio Psychology Press, P.O. Box 90095, Dayton, Ohio 45490. Copyright © 1991

Library of Congress Cataloging-in-Publication Data

Karnes, Frances A.
    Gifted children and the law: mediation, due process, and court cases / Frances A. Karnes and Ronald G. Marquardt.
        p.   cm.
    Includes bibliographical references and index.
    ISBN 0-910707-15-4: $15.00
    1. Gifted children — Education — Law and legislation — United States.
    2. Gifted children — Legal status, laws, etc. — United States.
I. Marquardt, Ronald G., 1939-   . II. Title.
KF4209.5.K37   1991
334.73'07915 — dc20
[347.3047915]   91-12061
                                                                    CIP

To

Ray	Sue
Christopher	Mark
John	Rick

Acknowledgments

Many individuals, professional groups and organizations, institutions and agencies rendered invaluable assistance from the beginning research phase of this project to the writing, revising, and editing which preceded publication. The chief state school officers, the state consultants for gifted education, and the state attorneys general were especially helpful and supportive as they responded to our many inquiries concerning mediation, due process, and litigation as means of resolving issues growing out of concerns about the education of gifted youth in their respective states. We are sincerely grateful to all of them.

The search for court cases and reports on specific instances of mediation and due process hearings began with inquiries placed in professional journals and newsletters. We would like to express special gratitude to the editors of *Gifted Child Quarterly, The Journal for the Education of the Gifted, Roeper Review, The Gifted Child Today, Gifted Child Monthly,* and to the editors of the newsletters of The Association for the Gifted and the National Association for Gifted Children.

Several computer searches, essential to the completion of legal documentation for this project, were conducted by Mr. Rae Turner, formerly of the law firm of Heidelburg, Southerland and MacKinzie and currently with Bryan, Nelson, Randolph, Land, and Weathers of Hattiesburg, Mississippi. We are indeed grateful to Mr. Turner and his associates for this important contribution.

We wish to thank the many parents, teachers, administrators, and colleagues interested in appropriate education for the gifted who were generous with their support and encouragement throughout this endeavor. For their skill, efficiency and patience we are deeply indebted to Lauree Mills, Tracy Riley, Linda Garner, and Tricia Clement, who provided expert secretarial and technical services in the preparation of this manuscript. Our gratitude is extended to Beth Franks for her excellent editorial assistance. Dr. James Webb and Dr. Patricia Kleine, of Ohio Psychology Press, have been patient, helpful and inspiring publishers. We are grateful to them for their editorial assistance as well.

Finally, we wish to thank Susan Marquardt and M. Ray Karnes, who not only provided encouragement and support for the project, but gave up their spouses for many Saturday and Sunday afternoons. To our gifted sons, Mark and Rick Marquardt and Christopher and John Karnes, we acknowledge that you inspired us to dedicate our time, energies, knowledge, and expertise to the completion of this book.

Table of Contents

Appendix

List of Figures

Foreword

Gifted Children and the Law:
Mediation, Due Process, and Court Cases

I am pleased to provide some comment to this unique and valuable book produced by Frances Karnes and Ron Marquardt. This volume, which reports and synthesizes the results of legal actions designed to aid the child with special gifts and talents, will be a distinct surprise to many persons who thought that court action was the primary tool for protecting the rights and ensuring justice for other types of exceptional children.

The provision of a free and appropriate education for exceptional children has often demanded remedies which extended far beyond the specific child and family concerned. In some cases these remedies were found in legislation, such as P.L. 94-142 (The Education for All Handicapped Children Act), and other times in legal decisions, such as the PARC vs. the Commonwealth of Pennsylvania case. The class action suits of the sixties and seventies allowed all children of a particular designation to benefit from a single legal action. In all of these instances, however, the children concerned were handicapped.

What Karnes and Marquardt have impressively demonstrated is that there are many legal disputes that have involved the rights of gifted children to an appropriate education. Part of the reason why the publicity about these cases involving gifted children and their parents has been largely lacking is that most of these legal conflicts have been settled at the state or local level. There is currently no federal legal mandate, as the authors point out, for the special education of gifted students, so the federal courts have typically not been involved, and a national spotlight has not shined on these issues. The Javits Gifted and Talented Students Education Act of 1988 provided demonstrations and research funds, by federal action, but no mandate for special services.

The frustration of parents who feel that their child is not receiving a proper or appropriate education is very real, and their feelings of hopelessness when confronted by the complexities and resistance of the public school establishment can be intense. The courts provide one avenue of potential satisfaction for their grievance, but, as the authors note, there are other methods, such as *mediation* and *due process* hearings, that do not involve the time and expense of a formal court proceeding but can also provide help to parents.

As is clear in reading this volume, the disputes reported here cover all aspects of the educational process, from eligibility to placement to appropriate programming. It is encouraging to observe how often the courts have decided in favor of the parents and the gifted child, confirming the rights of that child to appropriate education in a fashion similar to other exceptional children. Another surprise in the volume is how giftedness also shapes the results of other cases such as custody disputes and divorce proceedings. The type and amount of settlement is shaped by the presence of a gifted child in the family dispute.

This volume will be, in my opinion, a valuable resource and reference book that will be referred to for many years to come. Those who feel that strong measures are needed to obtain satisfaction for the educational needs of their children with special gifts now have a source book of enormous importance. Precedents and pathways have been established, so that one is not starting from scratch on such issues, nor should one feel totally alone. Almost certainly someone else has been there before.

The authors are to be congratulated on providing this unique contribution to the field of education of gifted students.

James J. Gallagher, Ph.D.
Kenan Professor of Education
University of North Carolina
at Chapel Hill

Introduction

During the past thirty years, litigation has forced great change in the public, parochial, and private educational systems of the nation. Judicial decrees have required school officials to revise their policies concerning racial and religious minorities, disciplinary procedures, and free and appropriate education for the handicapped. For better or worse, the battle cries of "due process" and "equal protection" echo in the nation's schools. There is no sign that the rush from the schoolhouse to the courthouse will cease.

Legal endeavors on behalf of gifted students are relatively recent, however, for several reasons. First, no federal mandate exists to identify and serve the most talented in our nation; only within the last decade or so have some states required services through legislative or state board of education action. In the past, the gifted child's needs were not as readily apparent as those of an oppressed minority or a severely handicapped child. Also, it was mistakenly believed, often with tragic consequences, that the gifted student, through sheer mental acumen, was a survivor. Today, there is an increasing amount of litigation filed on behalf of the gifted child.

While this book is the first comprehensive and analytical study on case law and hearing officer decisions involving gifted students, its purpose is to propose methods to *prevent* gifted education disputes from reaching the courts. Too often resources are spent trying education cases when the time and money could be more efficiently spent on the education process.

We wrote this book to meet the specific needs of many groups. Parents and guardians of the gifted who want more appropriate services in the schools for their bright children will find helpful procedural guidelines. For school personnel, the book provides a comprehensive source about the current status of mediation, due process, and litigation as it pertains to the identification, placement, and delivery of services for the gifted in public, private, and parochial schools. For lawyers and others working in the legal system, the book is a comprehensive and analytical document on litigation brought on behalf of the gifted. State department of education personnel, who need information on litigation as it pertains to state laws and policies and procedures in gifted education, will find the compendium helpful. Teachers of the gifted, both in regular education settings and specialized programs, who need to be well informed on all aspects of gifted education, will find the book useful. Concerned citizens, desiring a better educated nation, will want to know the legal action undertaken to provide appropriate services for the gifted, our future leaders.

In writing this book, we explored many sources, including information obtained from the Attorneys General Offices, the chief state school officers, consultants in gifted education in each state, as well as computer searches of current citations in education, psychology and law. Parents, educators, and lawyers from several states contributed other valuable sources.

Eight chapters comprise the book. The first chapter describes the current status of the state and federal statutes focusing on the gifted child. Chapter Two provides an overview of the court systems in the United States and their jurisdiction and function; selecting an attorney and devising funding strategies are also discussed.

The next three chapters contain an overview and analysis of selected court cases pertaining to the gifted. Chapter Three deals with judicial decisions regarding eligibility, admission, placement, appropriate programming, and other services. The fourth chapter describes cases on general school policies affecting gifted students and their teachers. Chapter Five pertains to decisions on tort liability and domestic relations as they apply to the gifted.

Chapter Six describes the mediation process for those who seek an informal solution to disputes brought on behalf of the gifted. The seventh chapter discusses due process and the hearings, by state, which have been conducted specific to various aspects of gifted education. Chapter Eight examines some areas in gifted education that need clarification, and therefore, may be subject to future legal activity.

The appendices likewise contain valuable information. Appendix A contains the full text of the Jacob K. Javits Gifted and Talented

Students Education Act of 1988. State Bar Associations with addresses are given in Appendix B. National and international associations focusing on the needs of the gifted are presented in Appendix C. The locations of the Offices for Civil Rights and the American Civil Liberties Unions are listed in Appendices D and E. The addresses of the state consultants in gifted education, the Attorneys General for each state, and the Chief State School Officers are listed in Appendices F, G, and H, respectively. Several journals and magazines are published in gifted education and information on them is provided in Appendix I.

Readers who find these chapters and appendices helpful and interesting, should also consult Karnes and Marquardt, *Gifted Children and Legal Issues in Education: Parents' Stories of Hope.* This book contains the personal accounts of parents who successfully resolved disputes involving their gifted children. These stories, as told by the parents, are heartwarming and inspirational.

We hope this book will be a standard reference for law, educational, college and university, public, private, and personal libraries. Readers should benefit from exploring procedural mechanisms, due process hearings, and court cases relating to gifted education. Most important, we hope that gifted children, who comprise one of America's most important resources, benefit from the ideas discussed in the following chapters.

—1—

A Survey of Federal and State Initiatives on Behalf of the Gifted

Six-year-old Terry possessed all the characteristics of a child who would have a highly successful educational career. With an IQ exceeding 130, an identified gifted ability in reading and mathematics, the chance to participate in the enrichment program in his school district, and parents who were extremely interested in his educational well-being, Terry's academic future indeed appeared bright.

Terry's classroom performance, however, indicated a disparity between his abilities and academic reality. The teacher classified his school work as "inconsistent" and his classroom behavior as "distracting," characterized by "calls for attention." Despite his participation in the 150 minute per week district enrichment program, Terry was bored with school.

Terry attended school in Pennsylvania which mandates by law that gifted students be identified and served by each local school district. Part of the school district's responsibility is to construct an Individualized Education Plan (IEP) for each gifted student; Terry's IEP allowed him to participate in the enrichment program. But his parents felt that Terry's instructional needs extended beyond the scope of the enrichment program, and argued for accelerated instruction in reading and mathematics. When negotiations reached an impasse with the school district, the parents requested, as provided for under Pennsylvania law, a due process hearing presided over by a hearing officer.

1

In September 1982 the due process hearing was held and the hearing officer decided in favor of Terry. After hearing numerous witnesses and hundreds of pages of testimony, the hearing officer ruled that the IEP segment of the law on gifted education in Pennsylvania meant that the focus of gifted education had to be on the needs of the individual student. Terry was entitled to special instruction in reading and mathematics. Fearing that all parents of gifted students would demand individual curriculum materials for their children, the school district appealed this decision to the Pennsylvania Secretary of Education.

After reviewing the evidence, the Secretary issued an opinion in April 1984 refusing to overturn the hearing officer's decree. Terry won, but the dispute was not finished.

Cognizant of the costs that could be involved in providing individualized instruction to students beyond the enrichment plan, the school district appealed the Secretary's findings to a Pennsylvania Commonwealth Court. The case was argued in April 1985 and an opinion was rendered in April 1986. Again Terry won — but the dispute continued.

The Superintendent claimed the Commonwealth Court had created a new handicap, "boredom," and the school district appealed to the Pennsylvania Supreme Court. The case was argued before this court in December 1987 and a decision was handed down in March 1988 upholding the decision first made by the hearing officer in 1982. The Pennsylvania Supreme Court agreed that gifted education must be individualized under Pennsylvania law and that the school district could not meet the needs of every gifted child by placement in an enrichment program (Karnes & Marquardt, 1988). The technical details of this case, *Centennial v. Department of Education,* 1985, will be discussed in Chapter Three.

Before gifted education advocates become too enthralled with Terry's case, several caveats need to be mentioned. First, Terry was fortunate to live in a state mandating gifted education and whose regulations regarding gifted education mirrored the regulations imposed by federal law protecting handicapped children. Had Terry lived in a state without such supportive laws, as the cases in Chapter

Three illustrate, he probably would not have won (Karnes & Marquardt, 1988).

Second, Terry's parents were obviously quite supportive and willing to spend the money required to fight the lengthy legal battle. Not all parents would possess the perseverance and resources to continue the struggle.

Third, the case typifies the delay that normally occurs when court action is necessary. In this case, six years passed before the matter was resolved. And although the precedent established by the Pennsylvania Supreme Court will be a binding precedent in the Pennsylvania courts, until challenged, most of the school districts in Pennsylvania will continue to serve the needs of their gifted students solely through enrichment programs. Economics dictate this school district response. Also, while lawyers in other states can cite Terry's case as a precedent, until other state's courts agree, the decision is only a binding precedent in the Pennsylvania courts.

Fourth, had the matter been resolved without going to court, the time and resources expended could have been used for educational matters, rather than spending thousands of dollars on fees for lawyers, court costs, and all the other expenses parties incur during a legal struggle.

Parents and other advocates for the gifted often find themselves in conflict with representatives of the school regarding educational opportunities made available to or denied a gifted child or group of children. These advocates for the gifted, encouraged by recent successes in securing legal rights for the handicapped, are turning to the courts to require local schools to develop challenging programs of high quality appropriate to the special needs of gifted children. Parents and their legal counsel increase their chances of presenting persuasive and defensible cases, and better serving the interests of the gifted child or children, if they are conversant with the federal and state laws as well as local school district and state department of education policies relevant to the issue.

As stated in the Introduction, the purpose of this book is to suggest ways that gifted education disputes can be kept out of the courts. Before we present those ideas, however, it is important to review the statutory and case law that currently affects gifted education. This will also serve as an overview of the difficulty of winning court cases on behalf of gifted children. The remainder of this chapter as well as Chapters Two, Three, Four, and Five will examine legal precedents in gifted education.

Federal Initiatives

This section summarizes the federal statutes and policies which have an impact on gifted education. These include laws governing definitions and identification of the gifted, development and availability of programs, research and dissemination of studies, and the training of teachers and support personnel. While we have emphasized federal laws with specific references to gifted education, we have also included more general educational legislation when it provides support for programs which make substantial contributions to gifted children's educational development. Later in the chapter we will review state laws, policies, guidelines and procedures relevant to the development and implementation of programs for the gifted.

National Defense Education Act (PL 85-864)

Federal resistance to the idea of participating in elementary and secondary education, or more precisely the reluctance of the federal government to become involved in providing fiscal support, is deeply rooted in the constitutional and popularly held position that education is a prerogative of the individual states. In 1957, however, a dramatic event abruptly changed American thought and action about the relationship between education and national security and the role of the federal government in American education. The Soviet Union's startling success in placing Sputnik in orbit not only shocked the scientific and technological world, but set off education alarms throughout America and the free world. From the halls of Congress to local discussion groups in rural America, serious questions were raised about our schools: What is being taught in elementary and secondary schools and how well is it being taught? What are the standards of performance? What goes on in colleges and universities in this country? How could we have been so poorly informed about the quality of American education? How could we have assumed United States supremacy in research and development? Even children expressed their concern by raising questions about the superiority of Soviet scientists and engineers over their American counterparts.

Sputnik sent a clear message: Education is vital to national security and defense. Sputnik, and the ensuing questions about the adequacy of American schools, stood as an indictment of the nation's entire educational enterprise. Assuming an educational emergency, local and state school boards very quickly increased academic requirements, especially in the sciences, mathematics, and foreign languages. Congress noted the many expressions of concern about national security and preparedness and passed the National Defense Education Act of 1958 (NDEA). In doing so, Congress broke from its historical position on federal aid to the public schools. The single exception heretofore was vocational education, which has enjoyed federal support since 1917.

While the language of the NDEA law did not make provisions specific to the gifted, the hundreds of millions of dollars authorized and appropriated and the additional millions provided to the National Science Foundation were for the clear purpose of developing superior instructional programs in mathematics, the sciences, and foreign languages, all thought to be in the national interest. Large sums were also provided for preparing and upgrading teachers and other professional personnel for developing and staffing innovative but rigorous academic programs — the kinds of programs the gifted find challenging, and at which they usually excel. The underlying assumption was that very substantial improvements in education, especially for students of high potential, would be required to regain and preserve the United States' leading position in the world of science and technology.

Elementary and Secondary Education Act of 1965 (PL 89-10)

Passage of the NDEA in 1958, with its massive appropriations, set the congressional stage for subsequent enactment of a series of laws. During the next three decades, Congress appropriated unprecedented billions of dollars to upgrade and support elementary, secondary, and higher education in America. The Elementary and Secondary Education Act of 1965 (ESEA) and subsequent amendments thereto, substantially broadened and extended the purposes for which federal funds for education could be expended.

While the NDEA emphasized programs of interest to the gifted, the far more comprehensive ESEA focused on education of the disadvantaged, in response to concerns expressed in the "Great Society" and "War on Poverty" campaigns. The momentum gained by the advocates for gifted education during the immediate post-Sputnik era, and sustained during the initial phases of our own space program, gave ground during the 1960s to concerns about civil rights and the education and well-being of the socially and economically disadvantaged.

Elementary and Secondary Education Amendments of 1969 (PL 91-230)

In the late sixties, various advocacy groups for gifted education became increasingly vocal and influential; in 1968 President Johnson formed a White House Task Force on the Gifted and Talented. Though a formal report was not published, the nationwide survey conducted by the Task Force attracted the attention of influential members of Congress.

In 1969, bills were introduced in both houses to require a federal definition of the gifted, and to provide support for states to develop and expand programs for the gifted as defined. In addition, the US Commissioner of Education would conduct a study and issue a report on the educational needs of the nation's gifted, including an assessment of efforts being made to meet their needs. The bills did not pass when first introduced; support to the states was not immediately forthcoming. Nevertheless, the congressional leaders who proposed this legislation continued their efforts on behalf of gifted education.

The study to be conducted by the US Commissioner of Education was proposed again in 1970, and resulted in a mandate in Section 806 of the Elementary and Secondary Educational Amendments of 1969. Dr. Sidney P. Marland, then Commissioner of Education, directed a comprehensive nationwide study and reported to Congress in 1971 as required by law. The document, known as the *Marland Report*, was widely distributed and influenced developments in the field for years to come. The *Marland Report* set forth the first federal definition of the gifted, which found ready acceptance and was adopted in one state after another and in the professional literature. It presented startling information about inadequacies in the national gifted education effort and included suggestions for appropriate action.

The 1969 amendments to ESEA also provided for "Provisions Related to Gifted and Talented Children." Section 806 of these amendments called for the states to develop model programs for the gifted and to employ leadership staff in their departments of education. These amendments also added gifted and talented children to the groups for whom programs could be made available and supported from funds allocated under ESEA Titles III and IV. (It was now legally permissible to support programs for the gifted from Title III and IV allocations, but not mandatory that such programs be provided.) Additional emphasis was afforded gifted education in 1970 by amending the "Teacher Fellowship Provisions" of the Higher Education Act of 1965 to include teachers of the gifted; funds for training teachers in gifted education became available.

The 1974 Amendments to Elementary and Secondary Education Act of 1965 (PL 93-380)

Acting on recommendations included in the *Marland Report*, Congress granted authority for an Office of Gifted and Talented, which was established in the Department of Education in 1974, and for a national clearinghouse to disseminate information about developments in gifted education throughout the US. Categorical funding for specialized gifted education was first authorized through the provisions of Section 404, Title IV of the Special Projects Act included in PL 93-380. The $2.56 million appropriated for fiscal 1974 was used to assist state and local educational agencies in developing programs for the gifted, to fund selected model projects, and to provide training grants for professional personnel. Although much larger amounts were authorized to carry out the gifted education provisions of the 1974 amendments, actual annual appropriations remained about $2.56 million for four years. While at first glance this figure may appear generous, the funding only provided approximately $1 per gifted child per year.

Education of All Handicapped Children Act of 1975 (PL 94-142)

While this federal law is specific to the handicapped, it is also important to advocates for the gifted. This statute gives fundamental guarantees to a specific group of students for the right to free and appropriate public education in the least restrictive environment. The precedents it sets have been employed successfully in many instances by parents and other advocates for the handicapped in seeking through due process hearings or in the courts to gain access to appropriate educational opportunities for handicapped children. The right to procedural due process, nondiscriminatory tests, and the individual educational plan guaranteed that laws for the handicapped would seem equally applicable to the gifted. This legislation holds promise of serving the interests of the gifted and talented equally well.

Gifted and Talented Children Act of 1978 (PL 95-561)

In 1978, this measure passed as Title IX-A of the Education Amendments of 1978, and essentially extended the gifted education provisions included in PL 93-380. Categorical funding for gifted education was continued in response to such findings, concerns and recommendations as those found in the *Marland Report*. When President Carter signed this title into law, authorization was granted for an appropriation not to exceed $25 million for that year; the limit was to be raised by annual increments to $50 million for fiscal 1983. Despite the sizeable authorization figure, the initial annual appropriation for gifted education under the new law remained at $2.56 million as provided under the previous legislation. The appropriation was increased to $3.8 million for the second year and to $6.28 million the next, but cut back to $5.6 million for fiscal 1982.

As provided in the laws in effect at the time, 75 percent of each annual appropriation was allocated to the states for development and support of gifted education. The remaining 25 percent was used as discretionary funding for such support functions as the national clearinghouse, research, innovative or exemplary program development, and training for teachers and other professional personnel.

Advocates for gifted education had little time to implement the provisions of the Gifted and Talented Children's Act of 1978. It was repealed when President Reagan signed into law the Omnibus Budget Reconciliation Act of 1981. Included in this document was the Education Consolidation and Improvement Act which converted the prior authorizations for gifted education and twenty-nine other programs into a single block funding arrangement and reduced the aggregate authorization by 42 percent. This put an end to the Office of Talented and Gifted and to categorical funding from federal sources of state and local programs for the gifted until the last year of the Reagan Administration. Local schools were left with the option of designating their use of block grant funds under the provisions of Title II, Part C, Gifted and Talented, but relatively few districts selected that option over the many other pressing needs for which funding from federal sources also had been sharply reduced.

Jacob K. Javits Gifted and Talented Students Act of 1988, Title IV, Part B of the Elementary and Secondary Education Act of 1965

Throughout the seven years following 1981, support mounted at the local, state, and national levels to restore the provisions for gifted education which had been eliminated. This support was bolstered by the dissemination of findings in such convincing documents as the 1983 report of the Commission of Excellence in Education entitled "A Nation at Risk: The Imperative for Educational Reform." Finally, in 1988 the House and Senate passed almost identical bills which not only restored but expanded and updated the provisions repealed in 1981.

In admiration of his vigorous efforts for quality education for the gifted and talented, the Congress honored the late Senator Javits of New York. The first sentence of this new law (Section 4101 Short Title) read: "This part may be referred to as the Jacob K. Javits Gifted and Talented Students Education Act of 1988." The first two annual appropriations made under the new law stand as further evidence that the Congress intended to renew national leadership for gifted education in America: $7.9 million appropriated for fiscal 1989 and $8.9 million for 1990. It is anticipated that funding will continue.

Currently the Javits Act is the basic law of the land with reference to gifted education in America. Thus, the major provisions of the Jacob K. Javits Gifted and Talented Students Education Act of 1988 (Javits Act) are presented here (the full text of the law is included in Appendix A).

While very similar in content and spirit to the 1974 and the 1978 amendments to ESEA which initially provided for and then extended and continued a national office of gifted education and categorical funding for gifted education in the states, the Javits Act places relatively greater emphasis on identifying and providing services for groups of gifted and talented children all-too-frequently overlooked: the very able but disadvantaged by reason of economic and social circumstance, minority status, or English language deficiency. This emphasis could have an important bearing on gifted education developments in the years ahead in that it presents a challenge, not only to program developers but to the professionals who devote effort to the development of nondiscriminatory, bias-free instruments and procedures for screening and identifying the gifted in these circumstances.

The rationale for this act can be inferred from the findings which comprise Section 4102(a) of the law:

(a) FINDINGS — The Congress finds and declares that —

1. gifted and talented students are a national resource vital to the future of the Nation and its security and well-being;

2. unless the special abilities of gifted and talented students are recognized and developed during their elementary and secondary school

years, much of their special potential for contributing to the national interest is lost;

3. gifted and talented students from economically disadvantaged families and areas, and students of limited English proficiency are at greatest risk of being unrecognized and of not being provided adequate or appropriate educational services;

4. State and local educational agencies and private nonprofit schools often lack the specialized resources to plan and implement effective programs for the early identification of gifted and talented students or the provision of educational services and programs appropriate to their special needs; and

5. the Federal Government can best carry out the limited but essential role of stimulating research and development and personnel training, and providing a national focal point of information and technical assistance, that is necessary to ensure that our Nation's schools are able to meet the special educational needs of gifted and talented students, and thereby serve a profound national interest.

The Congress, in Section 4101(b), expressed the consensus view concerning the broad purpose to which this Act should be responsive:

(b) STATEMENT OF PURPOSE — It is the purpose of this part to provide financial assistance to State and local educational agencies, institutions of higher education, and other public and private agencies and organizations, to initiate a coordinated program of research, demonstration projects, personnel training, and similar activities designed to build a nationwide capability in elementary and secondary schools to identify and meet the special educational needs of gifted and talented students. It is also the purpose of this part to supplement and make more effective the expenditure of State and local funds, and of Federal funds made available under chapter 2 of title I of this Act and title II of this Act, for the education of Gifted and Talented students.

The wording of the definition of the term "gifted and talented students" set forth in the Javits Act is, of course, very important in the interpretation and administration of this Act. The wording could also become critical to the outcome of any due process hearing or court proceeding involving persons on opposing sides of issues concerning gifted children and their education. The following is the first of the four definitions which comprise Section 4103 of the Act:

1. The term 'gifted and talented students' means children and youth who give evidence of high performance capability in areas such as intellectual, creative, artistic, or leadership capacity, or in specific academic fields, and who require services or activities not ordinarily provided by the school in order to fully develop such capabilities.

Not only does the Javits Act call attention in Finding (3) to gifted and talented children who run the greatest risk of being overlooked if from "economically disadvantaged families and areas" or if they possess "limited English proficiency," but makes the identification of and program development for gifted and talented children at risk by reason of economic circumstance and language deficiency the primary emphasis. The section devoted to program priorities, Section 4105; states:

(a) GENERAL PRIORITY — In the administration of this part the Secretary shall give highest priority —

1. to the identification of gifted and talented students who may not be identified through traditional assessment methods (including economically disadvantaged individuals, individuals of limited English proficiency, and individuals with handicaps) and to education programs designed to include students from such groups; and

2. to programs and projects designed to develop or improve the capability of schools in an entire State or region of the Nation through cooperative efforts and participation of State and local educational agencies, institutions of higher education, and other public and private agencies and organizations (including business, industry, and labor), to plan, conduct, and improve programs for the identification and education of gifted and talented students.

(b) SERVICE PRIORITY — In approving applications under Section 4104(a) of this part, the Secretary shall assure that in each fiscal year at least one-half of the applications approved contain a component designed to serve gifted and talented students who are economically disadvantaged individuals.

Congress passed the Javits Act with provisions for restoring the responsibility for national leadership in the development and improvement of gifted education in America's schools to the Office of Education. That intent is clearly expressed in Section 4104(c) which calls for the establishment of a "National Center for Research and Development in the Education of Gifted and Talented Children and Youth." Section 4102 reads in part:

The Secretary shall establish or designate an administrative unit within the Department of Education —

1. to administer the programs authorized by this part,
2. to coordinate all programs for gifted and talented children administered by the Department, and
3. to serve as a focal point of national leadership and information on the educational needs of gifted and talented students and the availability of educational services and programs designed to meet those needs.

Throughout the Javits Act, it is made clear that private school children and teachers may benefit from the provisions of this Act. One section is devoted entirely to this matter:

Section 4106. PARTICIPATION OF PRIVATE SCHOOL CHILDREN AND TEACHERS. In making grants and entering into contracts under this Act, The Secretary shall ensure, where appropriate, that provision is made for the equitable participation of students and teachers in private nonprofit elementary and secondary schools, including the participation of teachers and other personnel in preservice and inservice training programs for serving such children.

While the Javits Act does not make it mandatory that gifted and talented children be identified or that programs appropriate to their special educational needs be developed and made readily available to them, the components of the legislation offer interesting possibilities for moving gifted education forward in the nation.

State Initiatives

Federal statutes and regulations pertaining to gifted education relate to developments at state and local levels. Of more immediate concern, however, to parents, educators, and other advocates are the relevant state laws and state and local policies, regulations and guidelines. Those who urge that more be done in local schools to meet the unique needs of the gifted quickly learn that there are many reasons for turning to the laws in their respective states, as well as investigating the state and local policies and regulations under which gifted education programs are developed and conducted. Legal avenues are especially important when advocates for gifted education either suspect or conclude that the laws and regulations are not stimulating and supporting adequate developments at the local level, but instead are being used to set limits on what can be done to meet the special needs of the gifted. Unfortunately, minimum requirements tend to become maximum expectations in many local schools.

Overview of State Legislation and Other Initiatives

Since state laws about educating gifted students differ greatly and are frequently revised, it would not be feasible to present detailed information for all the states which would be of specific use to parties in conflict in a particular state or local situation. Instead, we have included an overview of legislative provisions and policies in effect throughout the country, as of 1990. We hope this will enable advocates for gifted education in a given state to review developments in that state and its schools in the context of what has happened elsewhere. More detailed information can be found in the two reports utilized in preparing this summary: *A Survey of the States' Efforts in Gifted Education,* a 1987 report to the Wisconsin Department of Education by Janet Boyle and Charlene Laurent of the University of Wisconsin-Stevens Point after conducting a national survey; and the report of The Council of State Directors for the Gifted, entitled *The 1990 State of the States Gifted and Talented Education Report.*

Prior to the initial Congressional action in 1969, only a few states had passed laws specific to the education of the gifted and few had issued policy statements and guidelines for developing programs for the exceptionally able. Although gifted education legislation was in its infancy during this period, much more initiative was exercised at the local level. During the years immediately following Sputnik more effort was committed to developing innovative programs in local schools than is suggested by the attention directed to gifted education by state and federal legislative bodies.

Even so, the several measures passed by Congress during the past two decades stimulated initiatives within the states. By 1980, more than half of the states had passed laws specific to the education of the gifted and talented; most states provided financial support to local districts in which programs for the gifted were developed. Even though the intensity of interest in gifted education has varied from state to state during the past three decades, all fifty states and the possessions and territories currently recognize gifted and talented education through specific legislation, state board of education decisions and policies, or state educational agency guidelines and regulations.

Another optimistic note is that pronouncements and proclamations made by governors and chief state school officers in a majority of the states have supported the proposition that special effort should be made to provide challenging educational opportunities, and make them readily available to all gifted and talented children. With the possible exception of one or two states, state budgets for education now include funds to support gifted education efforts in local districts, and at least one person in most state departments of education provides leadership for gifted education development in the state. In most states, at least one institution of higher learning prepares teachers and other professional personnel for careers in gifted education and provides supporting services.

State statutes and board of education decisions typically require state departments of education to regularly issue policy statements and guidelines which are useful to local school personnel in developing and implementing programs for the gifted. These documents usually include a definition of the gifted, criteria for admission to and retention in programs for the gifted, and the basis for state funding or reimbursement to local districts for a portion of the cost of special programs for the gifted.

Mandatory Provisions in State Legislation

At least half of the states have followed the precedent set by Pennsylvania in 1963, and more particularly the provisions of the Education of All Handicapped Children Act of 1975, to pass legislation making it mandatory to meet the educational needs of the gifted and talented within the state. Typically, such mandatory legislation requires (1) the state education agency to provide gifted education leadership and services, (2) that in every school district in the state the gifted and talented be identified, (3) that programs appropriate to their needs be developed, and (4) that these programs be made readily available to all children who qualify under the state's definition of the gifted and talented and satisfy the selection criteria.

But writing mandates on gifted education into the state law does not mean all problems are solved. Even in such states, not every gifted and talented youngster is identified, and even fewer have access to appropriate and challenging programs of high quality. As Sally Reis (1989) cautioned, "a mandate does not ensure anything other than a cursory response to an educational need. Even in the best-funded and most active states, gifted programs are seldom comprehensive."

State Definitions of Gifted and Talented

After the passage of the 1969 amendments to ESEA, and the release of the *Marland Report* in 1971, the definitions of the gifted and talented accepted at the national level became the basis for definitions incorporated in state legislation and in gifted education guidelines throughout the country during the next several years. However, the problem of phrasing a definition satisfactory to all is difficult and complex. Thus, definitions included in state laws pertaining to gifted education are often controversial and subject to frequent amendment.

Despite considerable variation in the specifics from state to state, the currently stated definitions of gifted and talented tend to include the following common elements: (1) high general intellectual ability, and (2) exceptional aptitude for outstanding performance in one or more of the basic academic areas of study. Additionally, definitions accepted in at least 37 states and in Guam and Puerto Rico include references to creative thinking and problem solving abilities, while these two territories and at least 32 states include outstanding abilities in the fine and performing arts, and 26 states join the territories in including leadership ability in their definitions of gifted and talented. Psychomotor ability, at one time rather common in state definitions, has been retained in the current definitions in only a small number of states and territories. Psychosocial ability and vocational aptitude have been added as a component in a few states.

Criteria and Procedures for Selecting and Admitting Students

The criteria and procedures for determining who is eligible for admission to programs for the gifted and talented should and will usually be consistent with the definition of the gifted and the guidelines in effect in a given state at the time. These criteria and procedures include: ways and means of identifying prospective students, the persons who may recommend them for consideration, the specific test scores considered, previous achievement records taken into account, and the school authority authorized to make the decision about admission of each nominee. However, the states vary even more widely with reference to these details than they do in regard to their respective definitions of the gifted and talented.

According to the earlier *State of the States Report* (1987), 17 states, plus Guam and Puerto Rico, required that scores on individual intelligence tests be used as a key factor in establishing admission standards; in 23 other states this was only a recommendation. Nine states and two territories included individual achievement test scores in the list of requirements, while half of the states only recommended their consideration. However, group or other kinds of achievement test scores were required in 14 states, plus Guam and Puerto Rico, and their consideration was recommended in 25 other states.

Seven states and Guam required creativity test scores be used in identifying the gifted and talented; such tests were recommended in 26 states and Puerto Rico. Two states joined Guam in requiring the review of leadership abilities, and 23 states recommended that such a review be considered in identifying students eligible for admission to programs for the gifted and talented. Consideration of exceptional promise in the visual and performing arts was made a requirement in four states, and 23 states recommended that abilities in these areas be taken into account.

Each of several other indicators of exceptional ability were listed as a requirement by a few states, and by several as a recommendation. Some of these additional indicators required or recommended are: past products, record of academic achievement, reports on other worthy accomplishments, and results on critical thinking skills and psychomotor tests.

Multiple indicators of exceptionality were often preferred over any single indicator. Several states required, and a larger number recommended, that three or more components be considered in the identification and selection process and that subjective and nonstandardized measures be considered along with objective, standardized test results.

The states also vary widely in their requirements and recommendations concerning the agencies and the persons to be involved in the development and approval of programs. Each state establishes eligibility and admission criteria, screens and identifies students, determines their eligibility, and makes final decisions concerning admission to specific programs for the gifted and talented. Sometimes primary control of admission standards is vested in the state educational agency, or this authority may be passed on to local school districts. Similarly, cutoff scores on standardized tests may be the only admission consideration, or broader and more subjective considerations might also carry weight. But whatever the screening criteria and eligibility standards may consist of, they should be clearly stated and disseminated. Requirements for admission are usually set at a level which permits from 2 to 4 percent, and in some cases as high as 12 percent, of the states's school-age population to qualify for admission to programs for the gifted and talented. Further, even though the minimum admission requirements may be uniform throughout the state, the percent actually qualifying for admission may vary widely from district to district.

Provisions for State Funding

The enactment of a state law pertaining to gifted education is a major step, in that legislation provides a legal basis for gifted education programs and supporting services, and usually authorizes the expenditure by state and local education agencies of funds from federal, state and local sources to develop and implement these programs and services. Funds from state sources, whether earmarked or appropriated specifically for gifted education or allocated from the state's general education fund, are utilized in all states to provide some level of support for gifted education programs and services provided by local school systems. The total annual expenditure for this purpose from state sources ranges from less than $200,000 in two states (Montana and North Dakota) to in excess of $5 million in 20 states and $87 million in one (Florida).

Under the provisions of various titles in several laws, federal funds in varying amounts have been utilized by state education agencies, institutions of higher learning, and local school districts from time to time during the past quarter of a century in support of gifted education developments. Support has come in the form of allocations of federal funds channeled through state educational agencies to gifted education programs in local school districts, and allocations to state departments of education for the purpose of strengthening their gifted education leadership and service capabilities. Direct grants have been awarded to colleges and universities for research in the field and to provide stipends for undergraduate and graduate students who prepare for careers in gifted education, and grants to local schools and institutions of higher learning whose proposals for innovative and exemplary program and instructional materials development gain approval.

Extent of Authority Vested in State and Local Education Agencies

As noted previously, decisions on student eligibility and admission criteria, curricular offerings, performance standards, and administrative strategies for meeting the needs of the gifted and talented are made differently from state to state. In some states, tight control over these matters is vested in the state educational agency, while in other states, local districts are granted wide latitude in developing and implementing programs under policies and guidelines as broad and general as the state laws permit.

The departments of education, however, are clearly most often primary. In 28 states departments of education define in some detail the standards which must be met by all local programs receiving funds from state and federal sources, while the other states provide general guidelines which leave responsibility for planning and decisions about details to local school districts. Fewer than ten state educational agencies and that of Puerto Rico require a specific curriculum or course of study for the gifted and talented students. Several of the states have established criteria and make provisions for recognizing programs of exceptional quality.

Twelve states require that an individualized education program be planned for each gifted and talented student. In ten of these states, essentially the same provisions which apply to the handicapped are followed in preparing the individual plan for the gifted. Several states have a formal policy and outline the conditions under which exceptionally able students may be accelerated on an individual basis by grade level or in selected subject matter areas. Other states employ this procedure under informal guidelines. In twenty-five states, authority is granted for students identified as gifted to enroll in school at a younger age than other students, while in several other states the policy pertaining to early enrollment is left to local districts. Departments of education in 22 states are empowered to authorize the granting of Carnegie units to students for completing advanced courses prior to entering the ninth grade. Eight other states permit the granting of Carnegie units prior to the ninth grade, but leave the decision concerning this practice to the local educational agency.

Statutes, Policies, and Guidelines in the Advocate's State

Clearly, in the absence of forceful national leadership and federal legislation mandating gifted education, policies and procedures vary dramatically from state to state. Again, the point is that it is essential for advocates in a given state to obtain and carefully study current laws and relevant state and local policy and guideline documents as first steps in pursuing the educational interests of gifted and talented children in a particular local situation. Needless to say, one must not rely on hearsay or on information from casual conversations when preparing to represent the interests of gifted children. Upon request, state and local educational agencies should provide documents which outline the legislative or legal requirements, the policies in effect, and the current guidelines, rules and regulations under which gifted education programs and services are offered in the state and local school system.

To summarize, there are several key components of a gifted education statute and states have taken different approaches in constructing such laws. Essential to any statute are the following items:

1. a definition of gifted and talented;
2. provisions for identification including nondiscriminatory testing and selection procedures;
3. procedures for establishing an IEP;
4. program options including related services;
5. evaluation of programs;
6. procedural due process including mediation and impartial due process learning;
7. provisions for awarding diplomas and honors for students finishing high school early;
8. requirements for school personnel;
9. financing provisions;
10. the responsibilities of local school districts;
11. transportation.

Two states, West Virginia and Louisiana, have exemplary statutes which, in many ways, approximate a model gifted education statute. John A. Grossi includes a proposed model statute in his 1980 monograph *Model State Policy, Legislation and State Plan Toward the Education of Gifted and Talented Students*. Because state statutes are regularly amended, Appendices F and H provide sources where gifted education advocates can obtain copies of their current state statute.

Prospective Developments

The Jacob K. Javits Gifted and Talented Students Act of 1988 provides the basis for high hopes for the future, and advocates for gifted education will most assuredly follow the progress made under the provisions of this new federal law. With interest in gifted education at an all-time high throughout the nation, developments are moving forward at an unprecedented rate. In this climate, more parents and other advocates for gifted education are not only finding the law on their side but general sentiments with them as they seek enhanced educational opportunities for gifted children.

Without attempting to anticipate the next legislative moves to be made at state and federal levels, observers of the gifted education scene will undoubtedly be wondering how many other states may soon be joining the twenty-five which have already made it mandatory that appropriate programs and services be made available to all gifted and talented students in their respective states. A related question, subject to speculation, is whether a move will soon be made to have the Javits Act amended to make the kinds of mandatory provisions which now apply to programs and services for children with handicapping conditions under PL 94-142 applicable to programs and services for the gifted and talented. The same purpose could be achieved by amending and broadening PL 94-142 to have its mandatory provisions apply to all exceptional children, including the gifted and talented.

With or without additional mandates, there are indications that influential people, lay and professional alike, are increasingly accepting the idea that giftedness requires a special educational effort and extraordinary creative and challenging program developments. The nation could never really afford to stand aside as all too many tolerated the assumption that, on their own and in one way or another, the very bright would acquire adequate preparation for life and achieve at the levels for which they have potential. There is a growing recognition of the necessity to identify exceptional children early and to provide them with opportunities for education of the highest quality all along the way. Those who pursue excellence in education are not likely to settle for less.

Chapter 1
References

Boyle, J., and Laurent, C. (1987). *A survey of the states efforts in gifted education: A report to the Wisconsin Department of Public Instruction*. Stevens Point, WI: University of Wisconsin.

Education for all Handicapped Children Act of 1975, 20 U.S.C. 1401 (1988).

Education Consolidation and Improvement Act of 1981, § 551, 10 U.S.C. 3801 (1988).

Educational Amendments of 1974, § 404, 20 U.S.C. 1863 (1988).

Elementary and Secondary Act of 1965, 20 U.S.C. 236 (1988).

Elementary and Secondary Act of 1969, § 142, 20 U.S.C. 863 (1988).

Gifted and Talented Children Act of 1978, § 901, 20 U.S.C. 3311 (1988).

Grossi, J. A. (1980). *Model state policy legislation, and state plan toward the education of gifted and talented students*. Reston, VA: The Council for Exceptional Children.

Higher Education Act of 1965, § 521, 20 U.S.C. 1119a (1988).

Karnes, F. and Marquardt, R. (1988) The Pennsylvania Supreme Court decision on gifted education. *Gifted Child Quarterly, 32,* 360-361.

Reis, S. (1989). "Reflections on policy affecting the education of gifted and talented students: Past and future perspectives." *American Psychologist,* 339-408.

State of the States Gifted and Talented Education Report (1987). Kansas State Department of Education: The Council of State Directors of Programs for the Gifted.

State of the States Gifted and Talented Education Report (1990). Maine State Department of Educational and Cultural Services, Augusta, ME: The Council of State Directors of Programs for the Gifted.

Title IV, Part B, Elementary and Secondary Act of 1988, 20 U.S.C. 3061 (1988).

—2—

The Legal Process and Gifted Education

Before discussing the various legal means used to solve disputes involving gifted children, we will survey the various components which make up our judicial system. In one way or another, all the topics discussed in this chapter are important when matters must be resolved using the legal process.

We are not suggesting, by any means, that all disputes involving gifted children be taken to court. In fact, we recommend that the formalities of the legal system be avoided if at all possible. Much time, money, and emotional grief can be spared if all parties stay clear of lawyers and courts. As discussed in Chapter Six and Seven, it is much better for everyone involved to solve the dispute through negotiation, mediation, or a due process hearing.

Still, as evidenced by the remaining chapters of this book, on many occasions disputes cannot be resolved without resort to legal arguments. Therefore, advocates for the gifted need an understanding of legal concepts, court structures, and legal terminology.

Sources of Law

Legal theorists suggest the following sources of law: (1) Natural Law, (2) Constitutional Law, (3) Statutory Law, (4) Administrative Law, (5) Common Law, and (6) Equity Law. Each source plays a varying role in litigation involving gifted children. While natural law and constitutional law and equity principles have not been productive causes of action in gifted education cases, as discussed below, each has had its role in gifted education litigation. Until state and federal statutory and administrative law is strengthened, all three principles will be used by plaintiffs in gifted education cases. The following examples explain the importance of each law source.

Natural Law

The Declaration of Independence and the Federal Constitution embody natural law principles. The concept that everyone has the right to life, liberty, and the pursuit of happiness, as discussed in the Declaration and the United States Constitution, is often referred to as "natural law" engraved large on the American legal landscape. The natural law argument could be made, albeit with little chance of success in today's courts, that a gifted child should be given the opportunity to maximize his or her educational talents. To allow otherwise, so the argument goes, would deprive the student of the liberty to develop his or her talents, diminish the student's happiness, and, in the long run, also deprive the student of intellectual and material property.

Constitutional Law

While the natural law theory is rather farfetched and has not been useful to gifted education advocates, many cases involving gifted children touch upon state and federal constitutional law. Constitutional law is highest in the legal hierarchy and takes precedent within our legal system.

Because the Supremacy Clause of Article VI of the US Constitution states that federal law is superior to state law, the US Constitution reigns as the supreme law of the land. As discussed later, both the due process and equal protection clauses of the Fourteenth Amendment of the US Constitution are often cited in educational controversies. School desegregation cases and challenges to state funding procedure, for example, normally rely on the equal protection clause of the Fourteenth Amendment. At the state constitutional level, many states have due process and equal protection clauses as well as a general educational clause which mandates that all children residing in the state have access to public education for a certain time period. Naturally, if the court accepts your constitutional argument, your legal position is quite strong. However, courts have not yet embraced the argument that gifted children have extraordinary protection under the equal protection or due process clauses of the federal or state constitutions, or under the general education clauses found within state constitutions. Frankly, for a variety of reasons, i.e., the reluctance of courts to embroil themselves in school operations and the lack of a recognized discriminatory pattern imposed against gifted children, it is doubtful that courts will ever provide extraordinary protections for gifted children through the use of general constitutional principles. But if a suit is being filed anyway, there is no reason not to play every "string on the fiddle" and plead the constitutional arguments. Some judge in some jurisdiction might be sympathetic.

Statutory Law

Laws passed by state legislatures (i.e., statutory law) have played an important role in gifted education litigation. Because education is a state function in the American scheme of government, the federal government has played a relatively minor role in supporting gifted education. Thus, most disputes in this area involve state statutory law as the states carry the primary legal and financial responsibility of providing gifted education programs.

A key factor in a gifted education dispute is whether a state has passed a comprehensive statute on the subject and the court's interpretation of that statute. Chapter One provided examples of the essential components of a state statute. Successful litigants on behalf of gifted children have often been able to rely upon a statute to buttress their position, rather than relying upon a general constitutional argument such as "equal protection" or "due process."

Administrative Law

When a state passes a statute establishing a gifted program, legislators often rely upon "experts" in state educational agencies to promulgate regulations establishing guidelines to operate the programs. These regulations fall under the rubric of administrative law. As long as they do not exceed the boundaries as established in the statutory law, they are as enforceable as any other type of law. In any gifted education dispute, it is always wise to have all pertinent statutes and administrative regulations in hand before proceeding in the controversy. In many cases, the administrative regulations promulgated by the state education department (see Appendix H), will address the issue more directly than the statute. State requirements for the screening and identification of students for a gifted program, including approved assessment instruments, for example, are often listed in the administrative regulations.

Common Law

A fifth source of law is common or "judge-made" law. When a judge renders an opinion, this law often becomes a precedent for other cases in that jurisdiction which have a similar fact-pattern. Common law has not been very important in the protection of gifted youth for two reasons. First, as they have in many other technical subject areas, courts have deferred to the experts in the operation of school systems. Trained as generalists in the law, judges have normally taken a "hands off" approach in regard to the day-to-day decision making of educational administrators. Second, when judges have rendered significant legal decisions in the area of gifted education, they appear to have been most comfortable when interpreting a law passed by the elected representatives of the people. Therefore, it is extremely important that all parties be cognizant of all applicable statutes when involved in a dispute.

Equity Law

One other source of law that needs to be mentioned is equity law. Arising out of the harshness of the common law in eleventh century England, equity law is described as an appeal to the "conscience" of the court. Even though all aspects of law may be against a party, the party can argue that fairness dictates an opposite result from the law than would normally control the situation. An example would be a gifted child who is seeking early admission to school. While the law might be clear as to the child's ineligibility for admission because he or she failed to meet the minimum age requirement, a court might rule that it would be in the "best interest" of the child to begin school rather than spend another year at home or in a preschool program. Considerations of equity, or fairness, would dictate that the child's educational needs be served. *Doe vs. Petal Municipal Separate School District*, discussed in Chapter Three, illustrates this legal principle.

Court Structure

The court structure in America is divided into a dual system. There is a federal court system that deals with cases arising out of provisions from the United States Constitution, statutes passed by Congress, and federal treaties. There are also fifty state court systems which address disputes arising out of state constitutions and statutes.

However, as Figure 1 suggests, cases arising in state courts may go through an issue metamorphosis and change from a state issue to a federal question. An example would be when parents initially file suit because the district refuses to admit their child to a gifted program due to a lack of funding, then later discover the program is being operated in a racially discriminatory manner. The racial discrimination issue would trigger the Fourteenth Amendment equal protection clause of the United States Constitution, and perhaps, allow them to carry the case from the state courts to the United States Supreme Court.

In our federal government system, the states are primarily responsible for education. Therefore, unlike cases involving handicapped children where a federal statute dictates that the state serve the educational needs of all such children residing in the state, most litigation involving gifted children takes place in the state courts. Major exceptions are cases involving the gifted/handicapped which fall under the jurisdiction of the federal law protecting handicapped children, PL 94-142 and the previously mentioned issue of racial discrimination.

As shown in Figure 1, each court system has a major trial court

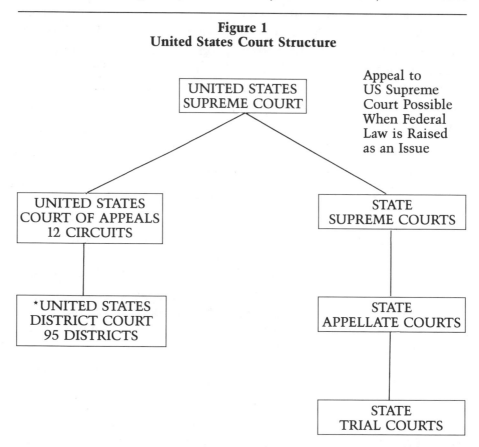

Figure 1
United States Court Structure

*The United States District Courts are the trial courts for the federal court system. If a gifted education dispute concerns a matter of federal law, for example, race discrimination, the matter would be filed in the federal district court. However, most gifted education suits will be initially filed in the state trial courts.

and tier of appellate courts. In both state and federal jurisdictions, the courts are usually suffering from an overload of cases — which means that if a dispute does reach the litigation stage, the parties are in for a tedious, drawn-out, expensive struggle. Often cases take years to make their way through the court maze, at considerable cost to the parties involved.

A typical dispute will be filed on the civil docket of a state trial court, and if not settled before trial, will go to trial before a single judge. Because of the costs and time involved, it would be rare to use a jury in this type of case. The losing party may appeal to the next higher court, and the case may eventually reach the state supreme court. With the exception of a few of the larger states, such as New York and California, most trial court decisions are not reported in the law reports. Therefore, most of the cases described in this book are appellate decisions which were important enough to the losing party to file an appeal.

Many state courts follow a doctrine that all administrative remedies must be exhausted before the judge will hear the cases. Therefore, if a school district and/or state has formal administrative remedies in place to settle disputes involving gifted children, these opportunities must be utilized before the court will hear the case. Settling disputes at the lowest level of adjudication makes sense, as it saves both parties time and money and helps relieve crowded court dockets. Several types of state education administrative remedies are discussed in Chapters Six and Seven. To save time, money, and possible embarrassment, litigants must make certain they have researched and utilized all administrative possibilities in their jurisdiction.

Figure 2 describes how a typical dispute might reach the courts. In this dispute, the parent has taken all the right steps to make the case ripe for judicial resolution. The parents first discussed the issue with the teacher and then proceeded up the administrative chain of command. In this example, the state provided for a due process hearing which the law mandated must be held before the matter could be entertained in court. After the hearing officer decided against them, the parents were free to take the matter to the courts. In matters where the due process ruling is against the school district, it may use the same procedure. As discussed in Chapter Seven, states have many variations as to what administrative reme-

dies must be pursued before going to court. However, Figure 2 is
typical of the procedures used in many states.

Figure 2
Steps to be Followed in
Resolving a Dispute in Gifted Education

Conferences →	Mediation → Meeting	Due Process → Hearing	State → Department of Education Review	Courts
Teacher, Principal, Etc.	(If Available) Mediator and Both Parties in the Dispute	(If Available) Hearing Officer and Parties in the Dispute Counsel (Discretionary) Student (Discretionary) Witnesses (Discretionary)	(If Available) Superinten- dent of Edu- cation or Designated Individual(s)	State Level unless Federal Law is an Issue

---

As many parents have discovered, a win at the trial level does
not necessarily mean victory. Because school districts are often
concerned about the policy and economic implications of a trial
court decision, the school district's attorney may take the case up
to the appellate courts. Figure 1 indicates that most states have an
intermediate appellate court and a state supreme court, but such
appeals are expensive. School districts are more likely to appeal as
they have the resources to wage legal war up the appellate ladder.
Parents, on the other hand, usually have depleted many of their
resources in bringing the matter to trial. Unless they are fairly
wealthy or can obtain financial backing from a support group, parents often cannot afford to appeal their case after an adverse trial
court proceeding. In discussions with parents who have brought
cases to court, a comment is almost always made lamenting the
expense involved in getting a case to its final destination.

Thus, it is extremely important who wins at the trial court level,
for several reasons. As mentioned above, time, money, and emotional
factors can be prohibitive in taking a case to an appellate court.

More important, appellate courts are reluctant to overrule trial judges unless an error was made in the interpretation of the law, or the trial judge's decision was against the "manifest weight of the evidence." The last standard is a tough one to overcome as appellate judges tend to defer to the trial judge who obviously was present at trial and could observe the demeanor of witnesses, and other important matters. Generally speaking, a gifted education plaintiff losing at the trial level will have a difficult time winning in the appeals court.

Selecting an Attorney

Few general practice attorneys have much expertise in education law. Obviously, school board attorneys have such expertise, but most private practitioners concentrate on real estate, domestic relations, tort, and business matters. Therefore, parents must be particularly careful in selecting attorneys in education cases.

It is also important that parents understand the financial arrangements with their attorney. The general rule in American law is that each side pays for its own legal counsel. In many areas of law, attorneys will be willing to take a percentage of the money recovered as his or her fees. However, in education litigation, the relief sought is normally not money but to force the school district or state to take a specific action.

Fee arrangements, therefore, are based on per hour or a flat fee basis. The flat fee approach has drawbacks in that it is often difficult to estimate how long it will take to get a case resolved and a lawyer might tend to overestimate the fee. On the other hand, a too low estimate could result in an attorney not pursuing the matter vigorously. The disadvantage of an hourly fee is its open-ended characteristic which leaves unsettled the amount of the total bill. Many attorneys use a combination of both the flat fee and hourly fee approach, initially asking for a set amount, for example, $1,000.00, and then charging a per hour rate, say $100.00, after the time purchased by the initial fees has been expended. Whatever approach is used, it is extremely important that all parties have a clear understanding of how the fees are assessed. In many cases, attorneys have a tendency to make such statements as "we will settle up when it all gets finished." When the bill comes, it is often an unpleasant surprise. Clients, however, must realize that the only commodity an attorney has to sell is his or her time — and that time is very valuable in the practice of law.

Clients should also ascertain what other costs will be involved in the lawsuit and who is going to pay these expenses. Costs such as filing fees, court reporter's fees, copying costs, travel expenses, and expert witness fees need to be estimated and assigned between the attorney and the client. Many of these costs will be absorbed by the attorney's fees, but some costs, for example the testimony of a psychologist acting in the capacity of an expert witness, are not generally paid for by the attorney. Again, the best policy is "no surprise endings" to a case.

How does one go about finding a competent attorney? Unfortunately, there is no easy answer to this question. The family lawyer may be satisfactory, but again, he or she may lack the expertise to engage in legal combat with a knowledgable school board attorney. Friends and business acquaintances are often willing to recommend an attorney they have used, but again there may be the expertise question. Also, lawyers, like physicians, provide personal services that require the trust and confidence of a client and one person's satisfaction may not carry over to another client. Another possibility for a referral is a state bar association (see Appendix B) or a national gifted association (see Appendix C). Bar associations often provide toll-free telephone numbers and attempt to match clients with attorneys. National associations for the gifted and talented have been involved in legal battles or at least have monitored court battles within their state, and these interest groups may be able to put parents in touch with attorneys experienced in education law. State codes of ethics make it unethical for an attorney to accept a case where he or she is not qualified to render competent services to the client.

While an attorney's expertise is important, the attorney and client must also be able to communicate well. Both the substantive and procedural aspects of educational law can become technical and the client must understand the case in order to stay in control. Good attorneys are extremely busy, but they must be willing to take the time to explain what is happening with the client's case. A hard-working attorney who is willing to work closely with his or her clients may be able to overcome an imbalance of expertise in the subject area.

It is becoming a recognized axiom in this country that the worst thing that can happen to a person is to be involved in a court suit. Much of the material in this book is devoted to alternatives to litigation. But as one parent lamented at a recent conference on gifted education, "sometimes you just *have* to go to court." Unfortunately, until there is better recognition of the needs of the gifted, this parent's statement may become a maxim in gifted education. Chapter Six relates how to better begin the process, but before getting to the more informal means of dispute resolution, we need to survey the existing case law in gifted education.

Chapter 2
References

Abraham, H. (1986). *The judicial process*. London: Oxford University Press.

Ball, H. (1987). *Courts and politics*. Englewood Cliffs: Prentice Hall.

Doe vs. Petal Municipal Separate School District (Unreported 1984 case).

Grillot, H. (1983). *Introduction to law and the legal system*. Boston: Houghton Mifflin.

Jacob, H. (1984). *Justice in America*. Boston: Little, Brown and Company.

James, H. (1977). *Crisis in the courts*. New York: David McKay.

—3—

Court Cases and Gifted Students'
Educational Opportunities

It is worth repeating: Litigation should be the last resort in disputes involving the gifted. Going to court is expensive, time consuming, adversarial, and emotionally draining. At a time when channels of communication should be open and utilized, turning the matter over to an attorney often results in a nonproductive period as each side researches their respective positions. Plus, the parties are at the mercy of the attorney's work schedule and the court's docket. As we shall see in the later chapters, it is much better, when possible, to solve disputes through informal means.

Nevertheless, there are times when informal negotiations, mediation, and due process fail and there is no alternative but to resort to the courts. The preceding chapter discussed selecting an attorney and a brief overview of the sources of law and America's dual (federal and state) court system. This chapter, and the next two, review cases which have been brought in behalf of gifted students and teachers in courts across the United States. In this chapter, cases which directly touch upon an individual student's education process will be discussed, and the next two chapters cover cases where the child's giftedness, or gifted education, was a related issue in the litigation. For ease of reading, cases in this chapter are further subdivided into the categories of admission to school, admission to programs, admissions and race, and curriculum modification.

Admission to School

Predating the current interest in gifted education were the cases involving early admission to school. In this section we will examine three early admission cases plus an interesting case involving gender discrimination. The early admission cases had different outcomes but are good illustrations of typical cases brought in this area. Optimistically, thanks to greater protection of females through the expansion of the equal protection clause of the Fourteenth Amendment, the gender discrimination case has only historical interest.

The early admission issue affects the child who is emotionally, academically, and physically ready for school, or an educational program, but who faces a statutorily imposed age admission barrier. Three cases, one from New York, one from Wisconsin, and one from Mississippi, typify such cases. The New York case, *Ackerman v. Rubin* (1962) concerns a student who wished to attend a special progress class offered at a New York City junior high school. Students attending junior high in New York at this time had the following curriculum options: (1) complete junior high in three years; (2) complete junior high in three years with an enriched course of study; (3) complete junior high in two years using an accelerated curriculum.

Options two and three were available to students who had achieved outstanding grades, who had been previously accelerated in school, and who were at least 11.3 years old. The plaintiff's son was admitted to the second program but was denied access to option three as he did not meet the board of education's age requirement. Although the student was close to meeting the age requirement, as he would be 10.7 years old by September 1, the board held fast to the 11.3 rule and denied him admission to the accelerated curriculum program. Having exhausted his administrative appeals, the student's father took the board to court.

During the court proceeding, the board readily admitted that the student was academically qualified for the accelerated program and that exceptions had previously been made to the accelerated section of the rule; therefore, the crux of the case became the adherence to the minimum age requirement. The father argued that the application of the age requirement to his son was "arbitrary, capricious, and without legal foundation." The board countered with the claim that the minimum age allowed students to develop emotionally, socially, and physiologically during the sensitive adolescent years.

The court agreed with the board and held there was a valid reason for the age regulation. The regulation, the court concluded, was based "on years of study and trial" and that the physical, social, and emotional maturity of children were proper concerns of educators. The father in this case was attempting to substitute his judgment for the judgment of experts in the field, the court opined, and the father, as well as the court, should yield to this expertise.

In rendering this opinion, the court failed to recognize that the presumption against admission of children below the minimum age could be overcome. This created an irrebuttable presumption which was not wise, especially when an agency of the state was involved. Such irrebuttable presumptions are open to attack under the Fourteenth Amendment due process and equal protection clauses which prohibit states from denying any persons these basic protections. What the court was effectively doing, in this case, was establishing a precedent for the state of New York which would prohibit all children, less than the minimum age, from ever being admitted to an accelerated program. A better approach would have been for the court to suggest that the minimum age requirement could be overcome by expert testimony as to the academic, emotional, and physiological age of the child. If convincing testimony regarding these factors was not presented at trial, then the age requirement would be controlling.

Early Admission in Wisconsin

Another age-related admission to school case, *Zweifel v. Joint Dist. No. 1, Belleville, (1977)*, involved Kyle Zweifel who was denied early entry into a Wisconsin kindergarten program. Kyle could read, write, spell, add and subtract, and education and medical experts predicted that he had already mastered the subjects taught in the next three grades. The five members of a multidisciplinary evaluation team found Kyle to be physically, mentally, socially, and emotionally ready for school.

Unfortunately for Kyle, he was only four and a half years old at the time. School district regulations required that children in the district be five years old by December 1 of the year in which admissions was desired. Although Kyle would not be five until February 4, 1977, Kyle's parents contacted the superintendent requesting admission to kindergarten in the fall of 1976. The above described testing was completed by the multidisciplinary team and the parents appeared before the school board in June requesting that early admission be granted. This request was denied and the parents, accompanied by an attorney, met again with the school board in July. This request was also denied, but the parents tried again at the August board meeting. While the results were the same as the two previous meetings, the parents' persistence resulted in their being given five reasons for preventing Kyle from attending kindergarten:

1. The school district would not receive state aid for Kyle's attendance;

2. The board did not wish to set a precedent for early admission cases in the district;

3. The board was worried about Kyle's social and emotional readiness for school;

4. The board was concerned about Kyle's ability to physically compete with his peers; and

5. The district had no gifted program to serve Kyle's needs.

Even when the parents offered to reimburse the district for the loss of state funds, the school district remained resolute and the parents sued in a local trial court for injunctive and declaratory relief. The trial court ruled in favor of the district and the parents appealed the case to the Wisconsin Supreme Court.

On appeal, the parents had two major claims to argue before the state's highest court. The first focused on Art. X, Sec. 3 of the Wisconsin Constitution which, *inter alia*, requires:

The legislature shall provide by law for the establishment of district schools, which shall be as nearly uniform as practicable; and such schools shall be free and without charge for tuition to all children between the ages of 4 and 20 years.

Two separate issues arose under this constitutional claim. Because some school districts within the state did provide for early admission, did the uniformity provision of Art. X, Sec. 3 require all school districts within the state to do so? And, did the explicit mention of age four in this constitutional provision require school districts to provide schooling for all four-year-old children?

Both issues were decided in favor of the district. The court concluded that the uniformity provision did not require school districts be identical with regard to services and programs offered. To ascribe to such a literal reading would result in a situation where every time a school district initiated a new activity, every other school district in the state would have to follow suit. Therefore, even though some school districts in Wisconsin admitted four-year-old children to kindergarten, the uniformity provision did not require all school districts within the state to grant early admission. Nor did the court accept the argument that because there was a statute which provided for early admission to the first grade in exceptional cases, the uniformity provision dictated that Kyle be granted early admission to kindergarten. Instead, the court concluded that Wisconsin law required an opportunity for early admission when the school district operated a kindergarten, but that early admission to kindergarten was clearly the decision of the school board, and in this particular case there was no evidence that the school board had abused its discretion.

In regard to the Wisconsin constitutional provision which reads schools "shall be free and without charge for tuition to all children between the ages of 4 and 20 years," the court held that the emphasis should be on the free tuition section of the provision. School districts did not have to provide for schooling for persons between those ages, but if they did, the education had to be free. In no way did this constitutional provision require the establishment of a kindergarten for four-year-olds in every school district within the state.

Two justices dissented. Justice Abraham in a dissent joined by Justice Heffenan concluded that the five reasons provided by the school board for not admitting Kyle could not withstand scrutiny. One reason, the fear of setting a precedent, meant that no child would ever be granted early admission. This was not congruent with the majority's holding that such decisions should rest at the discretion of the school board. The dissenters dismissed the second reason, that the district had no gifted program, as not being relevant in an early admission decision. The third reason cited by the board, that there was no state aid available, was also irrelevant; the proper question to ask, the dissenters claimed, was whether there were sufficient funds available, a question the board never answered. The other two reasons cited regarding the social, emotional, and physical development, the dissenters felt had been satisfied in favor of Kyle by the testimony at trial. But in this case, because it was uncertain as to which of the board reasons were controlling in Kyle's case, it was difficult to determine which standard the board had used to reach its decision. To make certain the early admission process is applied evenly, the dissenters urged the board to establish standards and criteria for making early admission decisions, and to disseminate this information to interested parents.

Early Admission — Mississippi Style

A more positive outcome for gifted education proponents was obtained in a Mississippi trial court case, *Doe v. Petal Municipal Separate School District* (1984). Because the records are sealed in Mississippi in cases of this type, the names of the parties must be kept confidential. At the time this case was decided, Mississippi did not have a statewide kindergarten program, and a child had to be six years old by September 1 to enter the first grade. Realizing their child was gifted but did not meet the chronological age requirement, the parents had the child tested at a local university. Test results indicated that the child was emotionally and mentally ready to attend the first grade. Negotiations with the school district were unproductive because of the state law, so the parents filed suit against the local school board. The attorneys for both the parents and the school board petitioned the court to enter a summary judgment, an accelerated process used in some cases to reach a judicial resolution. Using the university test results as a basis for his decision, the trial judge ordered the child to be admitted to the first grade. In Mississippi, the trial judge pointed out in a succinct, two-page court order, there was no "speedy or adequate remedy at law" as Mississippi had no statutory provision for early admissions for exceptional children. Therefore, when such admission was appropriate, the only remedy available to the parents was a court order using the court's equity powers. Subsequently, the father has garnered early admission to kindergarten through court order for two additional children in the family. The most recent case was decided in the summer of 1990.

These cases present a sharp contrast in the use of the courts to seek early admission for a gifted child. In the Wisconsin and New York cases, both the trial and the appellate courts were reluctant to exercise judicial power to grant admission, concluding that there was no abuse of school board discretion. Also, the Wisconsin courts were unwilling to stretch the applicability of the first grade early admission statute to early admission disputes involving prospective kindergarten students. It would have been easy for the Mississippi judge to act in a similar judicial restraint fashion and ignore the petition of the parents of the gifted child by strictly construing the statutorily imposed age requirement. However, Mississippi judges, like those in most states, follow the legal doctrine of deciding cases involving minors in "the best interest of the child." Fortunately, the Mississippi judge determined early admission was clearly in the best interest of the "Doe" children and granted relief from the age requirement statute.

Admission and Gender

Similar to the *Ackerman* case, lack of evidence also injured the plaintiff in the *Vorchheimer v. School District of Philadelphia* case. The plaintiff, in 1975, was a teen-age girl who had graduated with honors from a Philadelphia junior high school. Her school record was so outstanding that she, along with seven percent of her peers, qualified for admission to two of the designated academic high schools in the district. One of them, Central High, had been an academic high school since 1939 and had an outstanding scholastic record. The second school was Girls High, had been an academic high school since 1893, had an equally outstanding record, and whose graduates had distinguished themselves in business and government. Both of the schools were segregated on the basis of gender.

The plaintiff visited both schools, decided she liked Central best, and applied for admission at the all male school. Although the schools were similar in academic standing with the exceptions of Central's recognized superiority in science, Vorchheimer was convinced that she would be harmed by her three year stay at Girls High. She felt much more comfortable with the academic atmosphere of Central High. When she was denied admission to Central, she enrolled in George Washington High School and filed suit against the Philadelphia school district.

The first round of litigation brought victory in a federal district court. Basing her case on 42 U.S.C. 1983 which prohibits discrimination by persons acting under the color of state law, Vorchheimer obtained an injunction admitting her and other qualified female students to Central High. However, the victory was only temporary.

On appeal, the school district convinced the circuit court of appeals that the schools were of equal academic standing and prestige and that the key issue in the case was one of accessibility rather than entrance to a specific school. The court concluded that the plaintiff had access to a quality school within the district and that she presented no evidence as to how she would be injured by being denied admission to Central. The court's search for relevant federal educational statutes revealed no statutory prohibition of single gender secondary schools, and the lack of evidence as to injury made the court unwilling to stretch the equal protection clause of the Fourteenth Amendment that far. In fact, the court embraced the idea that segregation of the sexes might have some educational value and thus this disparate treatment of the sexes was permissible.

There was a very strong dissent in this case which found that the equal protection clause of the Fourteenth Amendment did provide Susan Vorchheimer a remedy. But the point is that the plaintiff should have focused on the specific injury she suffered by her denial to Central. Perhaps the strong science orientation could have been highlighted in the case or some other curriculum comparison that would have focused on the possible educational deficiency of Girls High. As might be expected, the appellate court was unwilling to second-guess education experts on a claim that the academic atmosphere at one school was better than another.

Admission to Programs

A New York case, which could have been a seminal case in protecting the gifted, occurred in the New Rochelle School District, *Bennett v. New Rochelle School District* (1985). This case provides insight into the difficulty of protecting a gifted child when there is no statutory mandate present in a state. It also illustrates the reluctance of judges to intervene in state educational policy. New York has a permissive gifted educational statute, and although the plaintiffs had a very strong case, several factors kept this from being a landmark decision.

The City School District of New Rochelle identified 109 students as eligible for their newly created gifted education program. Unfortunately for 72 of the students, the program had sufficient funds to allow only 37 students to participate. In an attempt to be fair, a lottery drawing was used to select the lucky 37. One eligible student's name was not drawn and her father, an attorney, brought suit against the school district. The suit had its foundation in both constitutional and statutory law.

The father unsuccessfully argued that the wording in the New York statute, "school districts of this state should develop programs to insure that children reach their full academic potential," required New Rochelle's program to serve all gifted students in specialized programs. Instead, both the trial and the appellate courts found the use of "should" rather than "shall" in the Education Law article controlling. Further substantiating the permissiveness of the New York approach, the court opined, was that New York law did not require any particular type of gifted program to be initiated nor did state law require programs of a specific size. The only requirement was that if state money was received to operate a gifted program, the money had to be spent on the education of the district's gifted students.

The New York courts also did not find persuasive the arguments that a statutory increase in funding for a program, nor an end-of-the-year balance, required a district to expand a full-time gifted program. Barring a showing of illegality, New York districts had a right, absent from any judicial interference, to allocate funds as they saw fit. The spending of funds was an educational policy decision and best left to the discretion of local school authorities.

An argument that all handicapped children had to be served by the district and that both the gifted and the handicapped fell under the special education classification also failed. The court pointed out that a separate section of New York law governed the education of the handicapped, plus federal law mandated such services be provided to district students.

The plaintiffs also presented several constitutional issues to the court. The first focused on Article XI of the New York Constitution which states: "the legislature shall provide for the maintenance and support of a system of free common schools, wherein all the children of this state may be educated." However, using precedent as the basis for their rationale, the court concluded that this constitutional provision only required a statewide system of education. In regard to specific students, the Article defined education as a "sound basic education."

Perhaps the best argument for the plaintiffs was that the lottery drawing was so arbitrary and capricious that it violated the equal protection clauses of the New York and the United States Constitutions. It would appear that the education of a child would be such a precious matter that it should not be left to chance; but the court, again citing precedent, did not accept the arbitrary and capricious claim. The court pointed out that lotteries had been used in school desegregation cases, and that education had not been designated by the courts as a "fundamental right." Therefore, New Rochelle authorities only had to show there was a rational basis, rather than a compelling state interest, to use the lottery system to accomplish a legitimate state purpose.

Program Admission Battles in Pennsylvania

A series of court battles in Pennsylvania provide an example of the difficulty of obtaining a court awarded admission into a gifted program. If there is an award for perseverance and originality in litigation involving children and gifted programs, this series of court actions should win the sweepstakes. The cases are important because they illustrate the types of legal arguments parents use in challenging a decision not to admit a child into a gifted program.

The three cases, involving the same family, took place in the Bensalem Township School District in the middle 1980s, *Lisa H. v. State Board of Education* (1982); *Doe v. Commonwealth* (1984); *Roe v. Commonwealth* (1987). Both the state and federal courts were brought into this extended legal fracas; the litigation, during its long history, involved several different issues. Most important, for our purposes here, was the variety of claims made on behalf of the students. The children were evaluated for the gifted program in the Bensalem District but were not selected to participate. In what amounted to approximately five years of litigation in the federal and state courts, the parent of the children was able to get a multitude of issues before these courts.

Pennsylvania constitutionally mandates that "the General Assembly shall provide for the maintenance and support of a thorough and efficient system of public education to serve the needs of the Commonwealth." Also, in 1979, the Pennsylvania courts had held that gifted and talented students were included within the definition of exceptional children (*Central York School District v. Department of Education*). From this foundation, the plaintiffs argued that they were being denied a proper education in not being admitted to the gifted program, and that the expenditure of monies on gifted education denied them educational benefits that could be used to provide them an "efficient system" of public education. However, the plaintiffs lost both arguments in the Commonwealth Court.

The first argument lost was on what is now a widely recognized maxim in education law, that when a state creates a public education system, a child has a right to have access to the system but not to a particular level of instruction. Students have a property interest[1] in the statutorily created educational system but, once in the system, they do not have a right to an individualized program of instruction. This judicial reasoning applied equally to the plaintiffs' argument that they were being shortchanged in their educational scheme because money was being expended on behalf of the gifted. The court refused to allocate finances, ruling that the state had fulfilled its responsibility in establishing an educational framework. It was left to the education experts to best decide how children should be educated within that framework.

Throughout the various stages of litigation plaintiffs claimed that the administrative regulations emanating from the Board of Education violated the separation of powers doctrine. If the gifted education program was to exist, the plaintiffs argued, it should be established by the legislature rather than being created by administrative regulations originating in the education department located in the executive branch. The separation of powers argument that one branch of government has exceeded its powers is often made by parties adversely affected by administrative regulations, but with the proliferation of administrative agencies in our governmental system, the claim has lost its validity in recent years. Here, the argument was not deemed persuasive by any of the judges; they found, under the Pennsylvania statutes, that the department of education had the power to establish standards for gifted education.

The petitioners' third argument was that the use of the Wechsler Intelligence Scale for Children-Revised (WISC-R) violated their equal protection rights because the test had been designed to identify backward children and was not validated for the purpose of identifying gifted students. The federal court pointed out that the petitioners did not constitute a suspect class and therefore the state only had to show a rational basis for including the test scores in the selection

---

[1]Property interest refers to an interest protected by the Fourteenth Amendment which states that no person may be deprived of "life, liberty or *property* without due process of law." Designating an interest as a property right gives the interest constitutional protection.

process.[2] A problem that plagued the plaintiff throughout the litigation regarding their constitutional claims was that they could not fit into a suspect class category, which heightens the level of protection under the equal protection clause, nor could they produce any claim which constituted a "fundamental" right. In fact, both the state and federal courts, in this litigation, continued to cite the United States Supreme Court case of *San Antonio v. Rodriguez* (1973), which holds that even education is not a fundamental right. Lacking such a constitutional underpinning, parents have a very difficult time winning constitutional claims in behalf of the gifted. Also, in this specific case, the court indicated that other criteria, in addition to the WISC-R, were used for admission to the gifted program.

Perhaps the most novel argument put forth by the plaintiffs during the course of the litigation was that exclusion from the gifted program violated their right to freedom of speech under the First Amendment. It was not a question of the plaintiff's speech, rather that they were being denied access to the ideas being disseminated in the gifted classes. While this was a unique argument, the federal judge claimed there was no mention in the petitioner's arguments before the court of any particular knowledge or ideas of which plaintiffs had been denied.

One final argument needs to be mentioned. The Pennsylvania plaintiffs, up and down the court ladder and between federal and state court levels, claimed that their exclusion from the gifted classes violated their due process rights. The courts agreed that the petitioners had a property interest in attending the public school, but they did not have a property interest in attending the gifted classes.

A procedural issue in the litigation was the plaintiffs' failure to exhaust administrative remedies before seeking a court remedy.

---

[2]Courts include persons who possess visible and unalterable characteristics and who have suffered a history of discrimination as a suspect class. Blacks in America constitute a suspect class, but no court has given that designation to gifted children.

Both the state and federal courts repeatedly stated that a proper procedure would be for the plaintiffs to assert their giftedness and follow the due process procedures available to them under state law for disputes involving exceptional children. Pennsylvania places gifted students under the rubric of exceptional children and therefore the administrative remedies available to the handicapped are also available to the gifted. In this case, the parents ignored those remedies and alleged that, because they were raising constitutional issues, they did not have to exhaust their administrative remedies before filing their complaint in court. Both the state and federal courts did not accept this view and, on several occasions, dismissed filings because of a failure to exhaust administrative remedies. The courts took the view that, until plaintiffs lost at the administrative review level, they had not suffered an injury and were not proper parties before the courts.

Analysis

There is much to be learned from the Pennsylvania cases and *Bennett*. First, the cases illustrate the difficulty in winning admission to a gifted program when the argument is based upon general constitutional grounds, such as equal protection or due process. Also, the courts give little credence to arguments that administrative regulations, promulgated by executive agencies, violate the separation of powers doctrine. As long as there is some statutory authority for promulgation of the guidelines, the courts will normally support the delegation of legislative power to the state agencies.

Likewise, claims based on a state statute, or on a constitutional provision which requires the state to provide all children a free public education, are not successful in the courts. The courts routinely hold that these statutes just provide children access to a public education, rather than admission to a special program and, finally, while it is a doctrine widely adhered to in the law, the principle that all administrative remedies must be exhausted before pursuing relief in the courts is worth repeating. Not only does this save litigants from being returned to step one after they have filed their complaint in the courts, but it would probably save the unhappy parents a great deal of time and money if they could win at the administrative level. Opportunities for administrative remedies are discussed in Chapters Six and Seven.

Admissions and Race

There is no doubt that a great deal of litigation concerning race and admission to gifted programs is on the judicial horizon. As discussed below in *Vaughns v. Board of Education* (1985), no matter how hard some administrators try to create a racially neutral gifted program, problems arise concerning the lack of racial diversity. To date, the cases concerning the gifted have, for the most part, been contained in broadly based desegregation cases. That is, the admission of minority students to a gifted program is just one of the issues in a multi-issue school desegregation case. This will not hold true in the future however, because as general school desegregation battles are won, minorities will focus on admission to specific programs. Following this round of litigation will be the counter suits alleging reverse discrimination.

Vaughns is an example where the gifted issue was immersed in litigation attempting to stop a community from operating a racially discriminatory school district. For some time, the Prince George County School District had been operating an all white school district in violation of the equal protection of the law clause of the Fourteenth Amendment. Remember that blacks and other minorities are treated as a suspect class in this country, and courts provide these minorities special protection. Also, because this case raised a federal constitutional issue, race discrimination, it took place in a federal court.

As part of the desegregation plan, administrators in the district had taken great care to make certain that minorities had ample opportunity to participate in the gifted program. In addition to the normal testing procedures used for admission, both parents and teachers could nominate students to the gifted program. To make certain that teachers were trained to recognize gifted traits evidenced by the minority students, they attended workshops on the identification of gifted students. To further insure all the bases were touched, minorities were included on the committees that formulated the recommendations for the district's gifted program.

Despite these precautions, the district's gifted programs were composed overwhelmingly of white students. This lack of diversity was challenged in an ongoing desegregation suit attempting to wipe out the last vestiges of discrimination in the district. At the trial level in the federal district court, the school district successfully defended the selection process in the gifted program. The court agreed that school administrators had taken all the necessary steps in attempting to establish a nondiscriminatory program. The plaintiffs had not met the burden, the court concluded, of showing that the defendants were conducting a racially discriminatory gifted program.

An appeal by plaintiffs to the United States Court of Appeals for the Fourth Circuit brought a reversal. Because the district had a history of operating a segregated school district, the appeals court stated that the burden of proof was not on the plaintiffs to show the district was conducting a racially discriminatory program, but the burden of proof was on the defendants to show that the selection procedure was not discriminatory. Therefore, the district court had used the wrong standard of proof. Judges on the appeals court were also chary of the in-service training programs used to train teachers to identify minority children who were gifted, and the case was sent back to the district court for a rehearing. As of the date, there is no reported opinion on the rehearing.

Gifted Program Discrimination in Mississippi

Montgomery v. Starkville (1987) is another example of a federal court desegregation case involving a gifted education program. In this Mississippi case, plaintiffs argued that teachers were being unequally compensated on the basis of race; hiring, firing, and demotion was performed on the basis of race; the district's achievement grouping was racially discriminatory; the program designed for above-average was being administered in a discriminatory manner; and the district's program for creative students was also being operated in a racially discriminatory fashion. A numerical disparity between white and black students enrolled in the PEAK program, where students were selected on the basis of scholastic performance, and the VIVA program, for especially creative students, set the stage for the battle over the gifted programs.

Participation in the scholastically oriented PEAK program required students to take the Stanford Achievement Test (SAT) and the Wechsler Intelligence Test for Children–Revised (WISC-R). Ifthe student scored within the top ten percent of the SAT and did well on the WISC-R, according to state criteria, the student would be offered the opportunity to participate in PEAK. Use of these test scores resulted in the following racial distribution in the PEAK program:

Year	Black	White
1979-80	2	45
1980-81	1	42
1981-82	1	61
1982-83	0	92
1983-84	0	98

To combat the disparity in admission of blacks to the PEAK program, the school district stressed that the program had been created with the help of a biracial committee and the WISC-R had been revised in 1978 to mitigate cultural and racial bias. However, the court held that the defendant school district had not met the burden of rebutting, by clear and convincing evidence, the presumption that the PEAK program was being run in a discriminatory manner and ordered the Starkville School District to revise the admission process. Specifically, the federal judge ordered the biracial committee to meet with the State Department of Education and compose constitutionally permissible guidelines for admission to the program. At the time of this writing, no such guidelines have been approved by the federal court according to the attorney for the plaintiffs.

The number of black students admitted to the VIVA program was comparable to the PEAK program. Nominations to VIVA could emanate from teachers, parents, administrators, or self-nomination. Nominations could be made for creativity displayed in the areas of art, dramatics, or writing. Following nomination, the student's work was submitted to a panel of judges for an eligibility rating. The panel, composed of educators or professionals in the subject area who are not regular employees of the school district makes its assessments without being aware of the student's name, race, grades, etc. Guidelines for judging the work are furnished by both the district and the state department of education. When a student's work has received the approval of this panel, it is given to a biracial Local Survey Committee. If the work receives approval from this committee, it is then submitted, for final approval, to the State Department of Education Regional Screening Team.

Despite this labyrinth of administrative safeguards, black admission to the VIVA program remained quite low.

Year	Black	White
1980-81	1	37
1981-82	5	80
1982-83	10	119
1983-84	6	107

Although the court obviously concluded that white students participated at a higher rate than blacks in the VIVA program, the court used the ratio of blacks nominated and blacks accepted to hold that the VIVA program was not discriminatory. For example in the 1985-1986 school year, black nominations to VIVA increased to 24 and all 24 students were selected. In the 1986-1987 school year, 36 out of 36 minority students nominated were accepted into VIVA. Evidently, this high rate of acceptance was controlling as to the court's determination that the VIVA program was nondiscriminatory in operation.

Therefore, the only victory for the plaintiffs regarding gifted education issues concerned the requirement that blacks be given greater opportunity to participate in the PEAK program. Because the plaintiffs lost on the employment and academic grouping questions mentioned above, the case was appealed to the federal Fifth

Circuit Court of Appeals. However, the district court decision was upheld on appeal, including the issues raised over the racial disparity in admission to the PEAK and VIVA programs.

Funding and Race Discrimination

A third case involving the issue of race discrimination involved the expenditure of funds for a program alleged to be discriminatory. In *Board of Education v. Sanders* (1987), the Peoria, Illinois school board brought an action against the state superintendent of education claiming that the state board of education had no authority to withhold funds from a program it had found discriminatory. The state board had received complaints that minorities were under-represented in the gifted education curriculum and conducted an investigation of the Peoria program. The state board of education subsequently found the program to be discriminatory and suspended funds to the gifted curriculum.

Peoria's school board reacted to the suspension by filing suit against the state board of education in the local circuit court. Major issues raised by the local school board in the suit included the following:

1. The state board's withholding of funds forced the local school district to establish an illegal quota system which would discriminate against whites and violate the equal protection clause of the Fourteenth Amendment.

2. The state board had no statutory authority to unilaterally withhold funds in this type of case.

3. The relief granted to the local district by the circuit court should be an injunction against the state board to prevent the suspension of funds.

These arguments were found so persuasive that the circuit court granted a summary judgment to the plaintiffs. The state board filed an appeal with the Illinois Court of Appeals for the Third District and in their appeal raised the issues summarized below:

1. The state board of education was immune from suit under the doctrine of sovereign immunity.

2. Plaintiffs had been awarded relief in the trial court under a

theory not properly raised in circuit court by the plaintiffs. The issue concerned whether the state board had ignored a statute which could have been used to challenge the Peoria gifted program.

3. State law did provide the state board with the authority to withhold funds.

4. Federal law, the Equal Educational Opportunities Act of 1974, prohibited the state board from providing funds to educational programs upon a finding of racial discrimination.

5. General federal rights statutes and the Fourteenth Amendment prohibit the expenditure of funds to programs after the discovery of intentional racial discrimination.

One by one, the Illinois Court of Appeals rejected the state board's grounds for overruling the circuit court's decision. Sovereign immunity did not apply as the action was for injunctive relief and not an effort to raid the state's treasury. Instead, this action was an attempt to obtain money already appropriated by the state legislature. Therefore, there was no new financial demand against the state which might trigger the sovereign immunity protection.

Points two and three in the appellant's brief were equally unconvincing to the appellate court. The court found no merit in the argument that the trial court granted relief on a point not raised by appellees in the trial court. What was at question here was whether the state board of education had the statutory authority to withhold funds (point three) and the issue of whether the state board followed the proper procedure to challenge alleged racial discrimination in school districts (point two). This latter issue is so important in all types of legal cases that it requires exploration.

The trial court emphasized that a statutory procedure was in place in Illinois which the state board should have utilized. This statute allowed that when the state board discovered a racially discriminatory educational program, the proper procedure was to send the evidence to the state attorney general for legal action. Courts are generally very reluctant to make a substantive decision outside of established procedures, and in some cases the lack of adherence to proper procedures allows courts to avoid difficult issues. In most instances, as in the case here, courts will refuse to act when a political branch of government establishes a procedure for relief and that procedure is not followed. In *Sanders*, the Illinois legislature had passed a statute that the court deemed applicable but which had not been followed by the state board of education. And not only did the board fail to follow the proper statutory procedure in place for challenging a discriminatory program, the court decided there was no legal authorization which would allow the withholding of funds from the gifted program. Therefore, points two and three of the appellant's case were rejected.

Points four and five, the federal issues raised by the board, were also dismissed by the Illinois appellate court. Taking a view particularly sympathetic to the state under our federal scheme of government, the court ruled that state agencies must look to state statutes for sources of power. A federal statute or a federal constitutional provision did not imbue the state with a new power such as withholding state funds. This was true even though the Equal Opportunities Act specifically prohibited discrimination in educational programs on the basis of race. Besides, the court concluded, a state remedy did exist but was not followed by the board.

Having one level of state appeal left, the board appealed their case to the Illinois Supreme Court. With only one justice out of seven who agreed the state board did have an argument based on federal and state law dissenting, the state supreme court refused to grant the state board's request for an appeal.

Race and Magnet Schools

Another legal issue stemming from school desegregation deserves mention. Sometimes a school board will try to retain white students in a school district after it's been desegregated. One of the tools to accomplish this goal is the "magnet" school where children who are gifted and talented are grouped in one physical location. Such schools have been generally upheld by the courts as long as they do not completely frustrate the district's school desegregation plan. Even in a case arising in a district which had a long history of school segregation in the deep south, *Davis v. East Baton Rouge Parish School Board* (1983), the magnet school concept was approved for the purpose of making desegregated schools "more attractive to students and parents and thereby minimize white flight."

Vaughns, Montgomery, Davis, and *Sanders* do not establish any great legal principles concerning discrimination and gifted programs, but they are harbingers of the future. Just as in admission to any competitive program, administrators must carefully avoid entrance standards which are culturally, racially, or gender biased. After admission guidelines are adopted, they must be constantly monitored to insure that no particular class of students is being prevented from participating in the gifted program.

Curriculum Modification

Many disputes involving a modification of the student's course-work have ended up in court. Once a student has been identified as gifted, differences often arise between parents and school administrators as to the proper educational menu for that child. Parents often opt for special tutors, grade acceleration, off-campus programs at the local university, and other enhancements which would aid their child's education. On the other side, school administrators charged with educating all the children in a district often plead that limited resources restrict the availability of funds for special programs for the gifted. There is an inherent tension present in these situations where the parent understandably wishes to maximize the educational resources for the child, and the district must live under budgetary restraints.

Two Pennsylvania cases illustrate this tension, *Scott S. v. Department of Education* (1986) and *Centennial v. Department of Education* (1988). Consistent in their results, both decisions reflect a middle-of-the-road approach to solving curriculum disputes. While the cases will be binding precedent only in Pennsylvania, courts in other states are likely to take notice of these decisions.

The Pennsylvania Curriculum Modification Cases — Scott S., Centennial and Gateway

Early in life, Scott S. was identified as a gifted child with an IQ of 163. Scott is particularly competent in mathematics, and by the end of his sophomore year, he had completed B.C. Calculus which was the highest course available for high school students in the school district. His individualized educational plan (IEP) for the junior year included advanced placement courses and honors science courses, but did not incorporate any mathematics class work. Fearful that Scott would lose some of his mathematical skills, the parents, at their own expense, enrolled Scott in the Young Scholars Program at the University of Pennsylvania where he could participate in a calculus program.

The parents also requested a due process hearing challenging the lack of a mathematics course in Scott's IEP. At the October 1984 hearing, the parents requested that the school system provide Scott with an advanced classroom mathematics course, or else reimburse them for their expense in sending Scott to the off-campus program. The hearing officer found the classroom argument to be the proper remedy and ruled that the district was not liable for the costs involved in sending Scott to the Young Scholars Program. When the district appealed to the Pennsylvania Secretary of Education, the Secretary overruled the hearing officer's decision.

Scott's parents then appealed the Secretary's decision to the Commonwealth Court of Pennsylvania. Despite an excellent brief filed in their behalf by the Philadelphia based Education Law Center, Scott's parents lost their appeal. The issue before the court was whether there was substantial evidence to support the Secretary of Education's ruling that Scott's 1984-1985 IEP was appropriate. Deferring to the experts, the court concluded that evidence presented at the hearing suggested that perhaps Scott had gone "too far too fast" in mathematics to the detriment of his other studies. Also, the court noted that testimony at the hearing indicated that Scott would not be completely divorced from mathematics as the IEP called for natural science and computer science courses in which he could practice his mathematical skills. Therefore, the court ruled in favor of the district.

In a letter to the authors, Scott's mother expressed concern for Scott's mathematics education as well as about the impact of the court's decision on society in general. Because Scott had skipped the second grade, he was only fourteen years old when he completed the sophomore B.C. Calculus course. Thus, his public school math education would end at the tender age of fourteen. She wrote, "We read in the news of Russian, Chinese, and others being far superior to us in math and science. How can we ever expect to catch up if we refuse to teach our brightest minds? What would happen to a virtuoso violinist if the violin were taken away for 2 years and one expected this person to again perform at concert level 2 years hence. Children forget." Scott's mother conveyed what many parents of gifted children have felt in the past few years — the system is often not sympathetic to the plight of gifted children.

Two other details from this case deserve mention. Although Scott had graduated from high school by the time his case reached the commonwealth court, the court did not find the case "moot" and rendered a decision. Some courts would have avoided the issue on the mootness claim, but this court held the case involved an "important question affecting the public interest which could otherwise escape review repeatedly" and issued an order. The court's wisdom in going forward should be recognized because often, unless you have a bevy of plaintiffs in a class action, the mootness factor becomes controlling in education cases.

Second, *Scott S.* cites *Centennial School District v. Department of Education*, 1988, as a precedent. In *Centennial*, the commonwealth court held that "a school district is not required to devise an education program which makes the best use of each student's abilities, but only to identify exceptional children and develop education programs appropriate to their particular needs." When *Scott* was decided, *Centennial* was percolating up through the Pennsylvania courts and would eventually become a landmark decision in gifted education.

Centennial touches upon the same major issue as *Scott* — the extent that a school district must go in maximizing a student's educational abilities. As discussed in Chapter One, Terry A. was identified as gifted in mathematics and reading. Terry's IEP included placement in a pullout program where the district's gifted children attended 150 minutes of gifted instruction per week. Terry's parents believed that he was gifted the entire school week and requested he be given special instruction in mathematics and reading. The school district refused and claimed that they were fulfilling their state-imposed gifted education obligations by placing him in the pullout program.

After negotiations broke down with the school system, Terry's parents requested a due process hearing. Agreeing with the parents, the hearing officer ordered the district to provide Terry with special instruction in mathematics and reading in the regular classroom but keep Terry at his present grade level. As in *Scott S.*, the school district appealed the hearing officer's decision to the Pennsylvania Secretary of Education. But unlike the *Scott* case, the Secretary decided in favor of the parents. The district then appealed to the commonwealth court which supported Terry to the extent that it upheld the Secretary of Education's order to provide him with special education in math and reading.

Worried about the costs of providing specialized instructional programs within the classroom for everyone identified as gifted, the district appealed the case to the Pennsylvania Supreme Court. Taking a middle-of-the-road approach, the supreme court gave each side a partial victory. Centennial School District did, under Pennsylvania law, have to provide Terry with an appropriate education, which in this case included special instruction in mathematics and reading. However, they only had to provide Terry training within the confines of their present educational resources. If the district did not have a tutorial program or an off-campus learning experience in place, they did not have to create such programs to maximize the student's learning abilities. The school district was required to do more than just place a student in a class with other gifted students for 150 minutes a week because Pennsylvania law focused on providing appropriate education for individuals. On the other hand, the court concluded, there were economic restraints on how far the district could go in meeting the needs of the gifted child. Each school district did not have to become a "Harvard or a Princeton" in order to serve the needs of the gifted children in the district.

Instead, the district only had to make available the curriculum presently in place to serve the special education needs of the gifted children in the district.

Centennial took six years to make its way through the Pennsylvania courts. Because of their concern about the costs of providing an individualized instruction for every gifted child in the district, the school administration evidently thought the prolonged battle worthwhile.

At this writing, *Centennial* is the seminal case in gifted education. For Pennsylvania, it is a binding precedent that informs school districts that a general pullout program will not serve as an appropriate education for some gifted students. Instead, if an IEP identified special areas which need to be served, a school district must meet those needs through individualized instruction. The district, however, can meet these needs within its current curriculum offerings. If the student's capabilities exceed the district's resources, the district does not have to initiate new programs to meet those needs.

For states who have placed gifted education under their special education statutes, *Centennial* could be argued as persuasive authority that a pullout program does not meet the educational needs of every child. Therefore, the decision could have broader application than Pennsylvania. But the decision contains an inherent contradiction. The purpose of an IEP is to identify the type of instruction a child needs to grow intellectually. If this determination is made, but the school district cannot provide the services, how can one argue the education provided the child is an "appropriate" education? *Centennial* is a step forward, but not a giant step toward meeting the needs of the gifted.

Centennial was cited as a precedent in the 1989 Pennsylvania case, *Gateway v. Commonwealth*. This case began while *Centennial* was advancing up the appellate ladder; *Gateway* used *Centennial* as the basis to file an amended petition. *Gateway* involved Eric L., a twelfth grade student in the Gateway School District.

Eric had been a student in Gateway's gifted program since the first grade. He was so talented in mathmathics that he had finished all the math courses in the Gateway system by the eighth grade.

His parents continued Eric's mathematics education by paying the tuition and transportation costs for him to attend mathematics courses offered by area universities. Eric accumulated thirty credit hours in mathematics by attending these college-level courses.

Because Eric had not had an IEP since the sixth grade, his parents requested an IEP for his twelfth year of study at Gateway. As part of the IEP, they requested that Eric's grades for the thirty college hours be factored into his overall grade point average (GPA) and a mathematics curriculum be part of his IEP. Unable to achieve these goals through negotiation with the school district, the parents requested a due process hearing. The hearing officer agreed with the parents that mathematics should be part of Eric's IEP and recommended that the mathematics courses Eric took during his senior year be averaged into his GPA. The mathematics courses taken prior to his senior year, however, would not be averaged into the GPA. Gateway appealed the section of the hearing officer's decision which required the senior year mathematics courses be averaged into the GPA. This was the only portion of the hearing officer's decision which was challenged, and Gateway lost their appeal to the Secretary of the Pennsylvania Department of Education who upheld the hearing officer's decision.

While the appeal of Gateway was pending, the Pennsylvania Supreme Court decided *Centennial*, holding that a school district did not have to provide instruction beyond the curriculum offered by the district. If the edict of *Centennial* could be used as a precedent in this case, the school district would not have to provide the costs of incorporating a college-level mathematics course for Eric as he had exhausted the Gateway mathematics curriculum by the eighth grade. Citing *Centennial*, Gateway filed an amended appeal with the Secretary, but the Secretary took no action on the amendment and under Pennsylvania law, the appeal was considered denied unless acted upon within thirty days.

Gateway then appealed both the GPA issue and the inclusion of mathematics in the IEP to the Pennsylvania Commonwealth Court. However, the school district again lost on both issues. *Centennial* was held not to be controlling precedent because the appeal on the

IEP portion of the hearing officer's decision was not timely filed. The section challenging the GPA issue had been appealed within thirty days as required by Pennsylvania law, but the amendment to the appeal concerning the IEP had not been filed within the thirty day period. The court concluded that although *Centennial* was not available as a precedent when the original appeal was filed, this did not allow the school district to escape the thirty day time limitation for an appeal. Just because there was no controlling precedent, the court held, did not preclude the district from raising the IEP on appeal to the Pennsylvania Department of Education.

Summary

Several principles can be discerned from the above cases. Bear in mind that, for the most part, these are state cases and will have precedential value only in the jurisdiction where the cases were decided. However, the cases do provide insight into the judicial treatment of several legal issues.

The admission cases suggest that it might be easier to garner admission to a school than admission to a gifted program. Although the cases repeatedly hold that education is not a fundamental right in our society, if it could be shown that it was in the "best interest of the child" to begin the education process, parents might be able to secure early admission to a school system. This would be true even though the state had a clearly established chronological age requirement. Judges realize that legislatures pass laws which must have general application and there are often situations where equity requires an exception be made. For such an exception to be seriously considered by the court, the parents must have evidence that their case supports such an exception. Evidentiary materials must include tests revealing the intellectual, emotional, social, and physical capabilities of the child to indicate to the court that the child could compete with older classmates. While some courts might be willing to open the door to early admission, the challenge is going to tax the parent's time and money. However, the private school alternative might be equally expensive, or might not be available in the community.

Once the child is through the schoolhouse door, judges are much more reluctant to order a child to be granted admission to a gifted program. The above cases suggest that judges are willing to give great deference to a school district's criteria used to select students for a gifted program. Litigants' reliance on general constitutional or statutory law requiring states to "educate all children within the state" has not been successful. Also unsuccessful are claims based on the open-ended "equal protection" and "due process" clauses located in federal and state constitutions. As long as the individual admission decisions have a rational basis and are not whimsical and capricious, judges appear reluctant to second-guess the educational experts concerning the methods and procedures used in the selection process. On the other hand, if the admission process involves a racial question or there is a state law mandating gifted education and no gifted opportunities are available in the district, judges certainly may be willing to intervene.

If gifted education is mandated by the state, are school districts at liberty to serve the identified gifted student population in any manner the district wishes to put in place? Depending upon the state, probably not. The principle of *Centennial* is that gifted education under the Pennsylvania law should be individualized and individual education plans should be developed for every gifted student. Therefore, a low-cost program of 150 minutes of instruction per week might be financially expedient for the district, but not address the educational needs of every gifted student. Yet, under the *Centennial* holding, school districts in Pennsylvania do not have to provide instruction outside of their existing curriculum to maximize the abilities of the gifted child. The IEP portion of the decision is quite rational and it will be interesting to see if any other states, through statutory or case law, follow the Pennsylvania model.

Courts have designated certain groups in our society as a suspect class of individuals and carefully monitored the treatment of these groups by state and federal governments. To be classified as a suspect class, courts have identified three criteria which must be met. The group must have a long history of discrimination, their condition must be unalterable, and the members of the group must be easily recognizable. Obviously, gifted children do not satisfy the third requirement. Without qualifying as a suspect class under present law, it is very difficult for gifted children to win cases in court unless their challenge falls under a specific state law which affords them protection. Thus, it ultimately makes sense for the gifted education issues to be resolved through conferences, mediation, and due process hearings, rather than the courts. Before going on to these procedures, we need to survey the case law regarding gifted education policies.

Chapter 3
References

Ackerman v. Rubin, 231 N.Y.S. 2d 112 (1962).

Bennett v. New Rochelle School District, 497 N.Y.S. 2d (72 Appellate Division 1985).

Board of Education v. Sanders, 502 N.E. 2 d 730 (Ill. 1987).

Centennial School District v. Commonwealth Department of Education, 517 Pennsylvania 540, 539 A. 2d 785 (1988).

Central York School District v. Commonwealth Department of Education, 399 A. 2d 167 (1979).

Davis v. East Baton Rouge Parish School District, 721 F. 2d 1425 (5th Circuit 1983).

Doe v. Commonwealth Department of Education, 593 F. Supp. 54 (1984).

Doe v. Petal Municipal Separate School District (Unreported 1984 case).

Gateway v. Commonwealth Department of Education, 559 A. 2d 118 (Pennsylvania Commonwealth Court 1989).

Lisa H. v. State Board of Education, 447 A. 2d 669; aff'd 467 A. 2d 1127 (Pennsylvania 1983).

Montgomery v. Starkville, 665 F. Supp. 487 (N.D. Mississippi 1987).

Roe v. Commonwealth Department of Education, 638 F. Supp. 929 (1987).

San Antonio v. Rodriguez, 411 U.S. 1 (1973).

Scott S. v. Department of Education, 512 A. 2d 790 (Pennsylvania Commonwealth Court 1986).

Vaughns v. Board of Education, 758 F. 2d 983 (4th Circuit 1985).

Vorchheimer v. School District of Philadelphia, 532 F. 2d 880 (3rd Circuit 1976).

Zweifel v. Joint District No. 1, Belleville, 251 N.W. 2d 822 (Wisconsin 1977).

—4—

A Case by Case Look at School Policies Affecting Gifted Education

This chapter takes a different approach to examining cases relating to gifted students. Rather than focusing on individual admission or curriculum problems, it contains cases dealing with school policies of general application to gifted students and teachers. Obviously, there must be a litigant or class of litigants to bring the action to the courts, but generally, the court's decision will affect several students or teachers.

For example, may a school system refuse to award high school credit for math courses taken by gifted math students at the junior high level? If a state has a mandated gifted program, must the public schools provide bus transportation to the public school gifted programs for gifted students attending private schools that lack a gifted program? If a teacher is hired to teach at a public school for the gifted and then transferred to a regular classroom position, is this a demotion to the extent that it violates due process unless a teacher is provided a hearing? In states where there are no certification requirements for gifted teachers, may a teacher trained in gifted education be replaced with a teacher not trained in the field, but who has greater seniority? While some of these issues have been decided by the courts, others are just beginning to move through the legal maze. Chapter Eight discusses additional issues on the legal horizon.

School Policies and Gifted Children

One of the more novel approaches used to obtain a quality education for their children was an approach used by three families in Illinois, *Davis v. Regional Board of School Trustees* (1987). The Davis family and two neighboring families lived in the Worden School District, which had an enrollment of only 215 students. The district lacked a gifted education program and could provide only the basic educational services. The lack of more specialized services was particularly acute for the Davis family, who had a musically talented child with an IQ of 160.

Realizing their present school district could never afford to provide the services their children needed, the three families petitioned to have their property, which totaled 160 acres, placed in the neighboring Staunton School District. Their property was contiguous with the new school district and the families frequented Staunton commercial and cultural establishments more than similar entities located in the Worden District. Although neither Mr. or Mrs. Davis worked in Staunton, they belonged to a country club and held church membership in the Staunton District.

When the three families applied to the school districts for what Illinois recognizes as a "detachment petition," both the Worden and the Staunton districts refused their request. This denial was taken to the local trial court where the circuit court granted the detachment petition. Both school districts then appealed to the Appellate Court of Illinois for the Fifth District.

The appellate court affirmed the lower court decision and issued an opinion displaying great sensitivity to the academic and social needs of the children. Noting that the Davises wished to send their children to college, the court cited testimony that indicated the Staunton district had a full range of college preparatory courses. Furthermore, there was a gifted education program in Staunton and an opportunity for music instruction beginning in the fifth grade. There was no doubt of the academic superiority of the Staunton District over the Worden school system in serving the bright student.

Also, the court noted that Illinois Supreme Court decisions allowed the courts to consider the well-being of the "whole child." Extracurricular interests of the children, such as sports and social clubs, could be considered by the court in weighing the demand for the detachment petition. Considering these nonacademic factors made the petitioners' requests even stronger, as the Staunton schools offered much greater opportunities for extracurricular participation.

Despite clear recognition that the best interests of the children indicated that they should attend the Staunton system, one can understand the policy of the Worden District in fighting the transfer of the property. A district of 215 students and an income of $471,353.00 cannot stand many student losses. It is perhaps more difficult to comprehend why the Staunton school would not want to embrace the new families, especially when one child possessed a 160 IQ.

Even though the Worden district did not have a significant tax or population base, the court still found the transfer of the property to have little effect on the Worden district. The property tax loss to the district would be 0.3 percent of the district's total receipts, so the economic loss would be insignificant. Nor did the court find convincing the Worden argument that to allow this detachment petition would set a precedent resulting in a flood of future petitions.

Staunton's arguments against the transfer were also financial and equally unconvincing to the court. It was true, the court admitted, that Staunton would have to assume the bonded indebtedness of the property being transferred, but the new district would also receive the property tax income and state aid payments for the children. When this case was decided it was difficult, the court concluded, to precisely establish what gain in income would be sustained by the Staunton District. However, the Staunton schools were clearly superior to those in the Worden District, and the gain to the Staunton District and the families in the detachment area surpassed the loss suffered by the Worden District. Because this was the standard to be used under Illinois law, as to the granting of detachment positions, the Davis family and their neighbors won their case.

Annexation Denied

Not as fortunate in winning an annexation battle were Terry and Joann Desmond who filed a petition requesting their property be separated from the Malta Unit School District 433 and be attached to the De Kalb Unit School District 428, *Desmond v. Regional Board of School Trustees* (1989). The Desmonds and others met with the regional board of trustees of the county of De Kalb, but their petition to join the De Kalb district was denied. In an administrative review, the circuit court upheld the board's denial and the case was appealed to the Illinois Appellate Court. The single issue raised on appeal was whether the circuit court decision was against the "manifest weight of the evidence." The appellate court upheld the circuit court.

At the circuit court proceeding, both sides presented evidence as to the academic advantages of both districts. Traci Desmond, age seventeen and a tuition student at De Kalb, testified that De Kalb offered courses in Spanish, journalism, and communications not offered at Malta. Also, because she lived five miles outside the city limits of Malta and in the De Kalb Township, Traci testified that it was difficult to maintain relationships with students attending Malta High School.

Traci's parents also testified as to the academic advantages of De Kalb for Traci and for their other daughter, twelve-year-old Courtney. Mrs. Desmond pointed out that after attending a gifted humanities class at De Kalb, Traci could sit for an advanced college placement test. Besides the academic advantages of the larger school, Mrs. Desmond also noted that Courtney, who suffered from rheumatoid arthritis, would benefit from swimming in the De Kalb school district's pool. Mr. Desmond testified that his family's social, work, and church interests were in De Kalb and that the educational advantages of De Kalb exceeded those of Malta.

While agreeing that the Malta budget did not allow special programs for the gifted, Malta's superintendent testified that 89 percent of the approximately one hundred students attending Malta High School (MHS) entered college and that the smaller class size at

MHS was an educational advantage. Perhaps most injurious to the Desmond's side of the case was the superintendent's testimony that Malta belonged to the Kishwaukee consortium. If a student needed to take an advanced class, the student could attend Kishwaukee College and the district would reimburse the tuition paid, as well as awarding academic credit for the college class.

After plowing through a plethora of procedural issues, the appellate court concluded that, in this case, the evidence was sufficient to sustain the denial of the annexation. Most convincing to the appellate judges was the evidence that educational opportunities were open to Traci at Kishwaukee and that more than 80 percent of the Malta graduates attended college. As to Courtney's medical problem, the court did not find any evidence that Courtney could not continue her education without the benefit of a swimming pool.

This case illustrates the difficulty of winning a case on appeal and establishing a precedent which is documented in the court reports. Operating under established procedural rules, most state appellate courts will not disturb a trial judge's decision unless the trial judge has acted completely contrary to the evidence placed in the record. In this case, the school district provided sufficient evidence to counter the appellant's claim that the trial judge decided the case against the overwhelming weight of the evidence.

Transferring property between school districts is an extreme method of gaining access to quality educational services. In most states, cases are built on the issue of transferring students between school districts. For example, if a child lives in a small rural district that lacks a gifted program, there is often an attempt to attend school in a city that offers special instruction to the gifted. Normally, the receiving district charges tuition to cover the cost of educating the child and both districts must agree to the transfer. Recently, this type of transfer has been closely examined for several reasons. The school district where the child resides will lose state aid payments and the transfers might affect the school's classification. In some rural areas, it might even affect the question of consolidation. For the new district, the tuition might not cover the expense of educating the child. Equal protection concerns, as they relate to race and discrimination against the poor, could also come into play. Transfers will be a sensitive area for the courts over the next decade.

Busing Gifted Students

School policy concerning bus transportation for gifted children was the issue in cases arising in New York, *Sands Point Academy v. Board of Education* (1970) and Pennsylvania, *Woodland Hills School District v. Department of Education* (1986). In the New York case, parents of children attending Sands Point Academy and Country Day School petitioned the court for an order compelling the Board of Education of New York City to furnish bus rides for their children. At this time in 1970, New York law left it to the discretion of the school districts as to whether bus transportation would be provided within the district. New York City opted to provide such transportion for children to public and private schools providing the distance from the pickup to the drop off point did not exceed five miles. The transportation scheme even included service to children attending private schools outside the city limits. Unfortunately for the parents of the Sands Point children, the academy, a private school widely recognized for its academic excellence, was 8.69 miles from the city line.

The parents attacked the five mile limit as being so arbitrary, capricious, and unreasonable, that it should be overturned by the court. Although they lost their argument in the Kings County Superior Court, Judge Louis Heller wrote an opinion very supportive of gifted education. Noting that Sands Point Academy had a national reputation for educating gifted children, which had been recognized by Congress, the judge took the legislators to task for, in his view, not supporting gifted education. He had "looked in vain" at the federal Gifted and Talented Children Educational Assistance Act for money which would assist gifted education. He was hoping to find "an appropriation of, say, a hundred million dollars to provide for the needs of our most precious natural resource, our gifted and talented young people." Yet, he further lamented, "superannuated chairmen of Congressional committees don't bat an eyelash while pouring untold billions . . . into the endless Indo-Chinese rathole."

In contrast, parents of private school children in Pennsylvania were successful in forcing the school district to provide transportation for their gifted children. Pennsylvania law allowed a dual enrollment procedure where children enrolled in private schools could also enroll in the district's public school special education programs. Because gifted children in Pennsylvania are recognized as "exceptional" and must be provided an appropriate education, the facts involved in the case would seem to be clearly in favor of the parents. The Woodland Hills School District, however, thought otherwise. They contended that their obligation to the gifted private school children was determined by the general transportation statute which stated that private and public school children were to be provided equal transportation services. Because the teachers in the district traveled to the public schools to provide instruction to the gifted students, the district did not provide midday transportation to the public school gifted students. Therefore, because the public school children were not bused, under the general public transportation statute, the school district would not have to provide bus transportation to the public school gifted programs for the private school children.

The parents of the gifted private school children filed complaints with the Pennsylvania Department of Education, which conducted an investigation of the district's transportation policy. The Department concluded that the district should not follow the guidelines of the general transportation statute, but rather the dictates of a separate, more specific statute, which required districts to provide transportation to special education classes. The district disagreed with the Department of Education's finding, and took the issue to the commonwealth court.

Using a fundamental rule of statutory law, the court held that when a specific statute conflicted with a general statute, the more specific should prevail. Therefore, even though the district was not providing midday transportation to the public school gifted students, the court ruled that transportation must be afforded the dually enrolled gifted students.

Certainly this case is a victory for proponents of gifted education. It protects children who are enrolled in private schools, yet need access to the advantages of a gifted program. Now that many children are raised by a single parent or come from homes where both parents are employed during the day, this precedent will certainly benefit gifted private school students in Pennsylvania.

School Policy and Teachers

Several cases concern the subject of how gifted education teachers are treated by school administrators. For example, when a budgetary crisis occurs, may a teacher trained in gifted education be replaced by a teacher not trained in the specific area, but who has greater seniority? Or, if a gifted education teacher is transferred to a regular classroom responsibility, is this a demotion to the extent that it should trigger the teacher's due process protections? Is an administrator of a gifted program similar to a school principal, or is the gifted expert more in the category of a classroom teacher? School administration policy on all of these issues has been tested in either due process or court cases.

A Seniority Dispute

The question of replacing a teacher with a background in gifted education with a more senior but untrained teacher was the subject of a Massachusetts arbitration proceeding (Renzulli, 1985). This 1983 dispute involved the Dedham Education Association and the Dedham, Massachusetts Board of Education. Because of a reduction in work force, the Board of Education had laid off a senior elementary teacher and retained a gifted education teacher who possessed an interest in, and special training for, teaching the gifted. Massachusetts, in 1983, had no certification requirement for gifted education teachers and, by state law, left the formation of any such requirements to the local school districts. Both teachers had elementary certificates, but the less senior teacher, employed as the gifted teacher, had (1) applied for the gifted position when the vacancy was advertised, (2) attended a special summer institute on the gifted and talented, and (3) been trained at the summer institute in the particular approach used in the gifted program in Dedham.

However, the Dedham Education Association, representing the teacher who had greater seniority, argued that seniority and the elementary certification should be the key factors in the retention decision and filed a grievance with the board. When the grievance was decided against the Association, the teacher's group requested that, as provided for under the terms of their contract with the Board, the matter be submitted to the American Arbitration Association. The American Arbitration Association decided in favor of the gifted education teacher.

In discussing this dispute, Renzulli suggested that when states do not have special certification for gifted teachers in place, school districts can take several steps to protect a less senior, but trained, gifted teacher. Among the steps taken should be (1) a carefully drawn job description detailing the training and teaching skills required for the position, (2) a listing of the activities involved in the gifted education program, (3) a gifted education program model and a description of the teaching competencies necessary to carry out the program model, and (4) documentation of program activities so that student accomplishments can be related to the teacher's gifted education training. If these steps are taken, perhaps a trained gifted education teacher's job can be saved despite the lack of a state certification requirement.

A Certification Case

A 1989 West Virginia case addressed the question of whether a school board could hire a noncertified teacher for a gifted education program when a state certified gifted education teacher had applied for the position, *Johnson v. Cassell* (1989). By statute, county school boards in West Virginia have the authority to make employment decisions, but the decision must be based on the applicant's qualifications for the position.

Robert Johnson held a master's degree, was certified in gifted education, and was teaching in a gifted education program in Berkeley County. When the vacancy arose in Hampshire County, he followed the proper application procedures, including an interview with the Director of Special Education in Hampshire County. To Mr. Johnson's amazement, the Hampshire County Board hired a noncertified, non-master's degree teacher, who was presently teaching within the district, for the position. There were only two applicants for the vacancy.

Johnson appealed to the state superintendent of schools, but to no avail. Johnson's suit filed in the local circuit court, seeking a writ of prohibition to prevent the school board from hiring an unqualified candidate, was also unsuccessful. However, Johnson appealed the adverse circuit court decision to the West Virginia Supreme Court of Appeals and won.

In fact, Johnson won twice. First, the appeals court concluded that the statute relating to employment decisions made by the board did not allow the board to act in an "arbitrary and capricious" manner. In this case, the court discovered that there was such a wide discrepancy between the qualifications of the candidates that the board had exceeded its legitimate powers by not hiring Johnson. The court found unpersuasive the fact that the board had been able to secure temporary certification for the person hired.

Second, the court allowed Johnson's request for a writ of prohibition to go through a metamorphosis on appeal and treated his request as a writ of mandamus. A writ of mandamus is an order from a court requiring a public official to perform a specific act. In this case, the act was to hire Johnson as a gifted education teacher in the Hampshire County School District. Therefore, the circuit court decision was reversed and the case was remanded (returned) to the circuit court with the instruction to issue the writ of mandamus.

Obviously, this is an important court decision in the gifted education field. While its value as a precedent is limited to West Virginia, the *Johnson* decision provides a clear signal to other courts that when hiring decisions are required by statute to be based on qualification, a certified teacher should be given preference over a noncertified teacher — even if the noncertified teacher has seniority within the district.

Analysis

Because many states do not have a certification requirement for gifted teachers, these teachers, like the music or physical education teachers, are often the first persons relieved of their duties when a financial emergency hits the school district. The district can then place a teacher with greater seniority in the gifted education classroom and have that teacher handle both his or her old assignment as well as the gifted education responsibility. Obviously, this destroys any continuity in the program and most likely would result in a deterioration of instruction.

The simple legal resolution to this problem is for states to require certification and endorsement of gifted education teachers. This assures parents that teachers in gifted education programs meet minimal standards of training and provides teachers with some degree of job security. Otherwise, gifted teachers could find themselves in a situation where they joined a school staff, established a gifted program, and then were replaced by untrained instructors. The certification process prevents such a scenario from occurring as only a certified teacher could be used in the gifted program.

But as with most issues, there is a valid argument on the side of not requiring certification. One would hate to see school districts refrain from starting a gifted program because of a lack of certified teachers. Also, some teachers may be excellent in the area of gifted education, but for one reason or another, not able to pick up the courses required for certification. However, both of these problems could legally be handled by a state phasing in a certification requirement and allowing teachers who were interested in doing so to meet the requirements by an established deadline. It would seem that if there are certification requirements for teaching physical education, typing, and auto mechanics, states would be on safer legal grounds to also require certification in gifted education.

Transfer

A New Orleans case perfectly illustrates the frustrations of a teacher transferred out of a gifted instructional setting to a regular classroom assignment. The legal issue in *Rosenthal v. Orleans Parish School Board* (1968) was whether the transfer of a teacher from Franklin High School, which had a minimum IQ requirement for its students, to Easton High School, which had no such requirement, constituted a "demotion" and a "removal from office" which triggered the protections of the Louisiana Teachers' Tenure Act. These protections required the allegations against a teacher to be in writing and provided an opportunity for a hearing for the teacher to contest the charges. Neither protection was provided in this case.

Carolyn Rosenthal, a biology teacher at Franklin High School, was evidently a rigorous grader. Despite a conference with school administrators, Ms. Rosenthal continued to give grades far below the norm for that school. She did not believe her academic expectations were unreasonable, but the school administrators disagreed and determined that it was in the best interest of the district to transfer her to Easton High School. She would still teach biology, and receive the same amount of compensation in her new position.

Labeling the transfer as a demotion without an opportunity to be heard, Ms. Rosenthal successfully challenged the transfer. The Civil District Court issued an injunction prohibiting the transfer until the school board provided her with the charges against her, and the board found her guilty of those allegations. Treating the transfer as a removal from office, the district court issued a permanent injunction against the board until Ms. Rosenthal was provided a written list of charges and a hearing. Arguing the transfer was not a demotion, the school board appealed the injunction to the Louisiana Court of Appeals.

At the appellate level, the school board claimed, *inter alia*, that under Louisiana law, the board had the power to transfer or reassign teachers in the "best interest of the pupils and the system." The board's other major argument was that the transfer to another position of equal rank and compensation did not constitute a demotion. To provide support for this claim, the board had, at the district level, produced ample testimony that all teachers within the Orleans Parish District were equal in status and dignity.

Although the appellate court bought the idea that a demotion could constitute a removal from office and afford a teacher the protection of the Teachers' Tenure Act, the court did not find the tenure act applied in this case. Instead, noting in particular that testimony of the superintendent of the New Orleans Public Schools, the court majority concluded that the two teaching positions were of equal rank and dignity and did not lower Ms. Rosenthal's professional standing. To treat the transfer as a demotion, reasoned the court, would mean that no teacher who objected could ever be transferred from the school housing students with high intelligence test scores to another school without going through the formal procedures of the tenure act. Such a restraint on the placement of teachers within the system would be an unwarranted restriction upon administrative power. The court pointed out that this would be particularly true in this case as there were no special requirements for the faculty to teach at Franklin High School.

One justice on the appellate court dissented. Cutting through what he described as the school district's "legalistic mumbo jumbo," Justice Regan stated in his dissent that Ms. Rosenthal's transfer was, in reality, a disciplinary action. She had refused to change her grading standards, and therefore she was penalized by being subject to a transfer. Because the transfer was actually a punishment, the dissenting justice argued that she was entitled to the protection of the tenure act.

Legally, Ms. Rosenthal would have been in a much stronger position had Louisiana required teachers in the special schools to meet gifted education certification requirements. Or, she would have had a stronger case if the Orleans Parish School District had established specific job requirements to teach in their schools for high achievers. Without such requirements, her case balanced on the court's acceptance, or nonacceptance, of the opposing party's expert testimony that all teaching positions in the district possessed equal status. While she evidently strongly believed that she, professionally, was in a much better position at a school for high IQ students, she had little evidence to counter the expert testimony of the opposition.

Reduction of Teaching Assignment

Teacher demotion was also the subject matter of the 1982 Pennsylvania case, *Green v. Jenkintown School District*. In this case a teacher of the gifted, because of a decline in enrollment in her classes, was reduced to a 40 percent teaching load with a commensurate reduction in pay while less senior and nontenured teachers did not suffer any reduction.

Perusal of the facts of the case suggest that Green had a sound legal basis for initating the court suit. She had exhausted her administrative remedies by requesting a hearing before the district's board of directors and appealing their unfavorable decision to the secretary of education. Losing at the second level of administrative appeal, she had properly filed her suit in the Commonwealth Court of Pennsylvania. Both the dictates of Pennsylvania court precedent and statutory law appeared to be on her side.

Section 11.25 of the Pennsylvania Code requires a school district, in cases of teacher realignment, to allow "senior employees when properly certificated . . . to be allowed to fill positions held by less senior employees." A precedent, *Shestach v. General Braddock Area School District* (1981), had interpreted the statute narrowly and reaffirmed the protections of tenured teachers. As a senior, tenured, and certificated elementary teacher, one can understand why Ms. Green decided to pursue the case.

However, there was one fatal flaw in the case. Her case was based, not on Sec. 11.25, but on the demotion section of the code, 11.51.

Unfortunately for Green, demotions under 11.51 were treated by Pennsylvania law as being presumptively valid and the only way to defeat the presumption was to show that the demotion was arbitrary, capricious, or discriminatory. Because the demotion was based on a lack of enrollment in her classes, the court held the reduction in teaching load reasonable and not arbitrary.

A second tenet in the court's opinion was that the court was reluctant to disrupt programs by replacing a teacher with the more senior tenured Green. While the court did not go into detail regarding this issue, it appears, from the court's opinion, that the judges were reluctant to become school personnel administrators through judicial fiat. Had Green been able to make the case that the enrollment loss had forced a district realignment of teachers, undoubtedly she would have been in a much better legal position. The loss of students question, however, seemed only applicable to Green's classes.

Improper Suspension

In a case four years after *Green, Rosen v. Montgomery County Intermediate Unit No. 23* (1985), two tenured teachers in a gifted student program in Montgomery County, Pennsylvania won a significant court victory When the gifted programs in that school district were transferred back to the local schools from an intermediate unit, Janet Rosen and Phoebe Baxter were suspended from their tenured positions in the gifted program. The teachers appealed their suspensions to the school board and the local Court of Common Pleas and finally to the Commonwealth Court of Pennsylvania. The teacher's perseverance was rewarded at the commonwealth court level.

There was no question in the case that Pennsylvania state law allowed board suspensions when a decline in student enrollment dictated teacher layoffs. However, the motivation for the suspension here was financial: the board decided that because of changes in school funding, it would be more economical to return the gifted programs to the local school districts. Therefore, the teacher suspensions were caused by an economically motivated reorganization, rather than an actual decline in enrollment.

Taking the suspensions out of the decline in enrollment category put the case in a completely different legal context. Under Pennsylvania law, school boards had unilateral power to suspend teachers during periods of decreasing enrollment, but a different law applied when the board recommended an alteration of an educational program. Reorganizations of educational programs had to be approved by the Pennsylvania Department of Public Instruction. In this case, the Montgomery system had not sought the state's approval for its reorganization of the gifted program and, therefore, the teachers had been prematurely suspended. To remedy matters, the court ordered reinstatement of the two teachers and the payment of back salary and benefits.

Teacher Unions and Gifted Education

Two recent cases touched upon matters relating to unions and teachers in gifted education. A 1986 Michigan case, *Michigan Education Association v. Clare-Gladwin Intermediate School District*, examined the issue of whether a coordinator for a gifted and talented education program was a supervisory position, or whether the position should be classified as a regular teaching position and therefore represented by the union. The Michigan Employment Relations Commission designated the coordinator as a supervisor and the Michigan Education Association, representing the teachers, appealed the Commission's decision to the Michigan Court of Appeals.

Despite the fact that the duties of the position were still evolving at the time of the decisions, both the Commission and the court of appeals placed great emphasis in their determinations on the responsibilities of the coordinator. These duties included identifying gifted students, supervising the secretary, and generally administering the gifted–talented program. However, the central issue concerned the coordinator's role in hiring and supervising personnel for the gifted and talented program.

Personnel hired for the specialized program were initially screened by a committee of teachers and parents with the recommendations going to the coordinator. The coordinator would then select an applicant and nominate the candidate for approval by the superintendent. If the nominee met the superintendent's approval, the candidate was recommended to the board of education. Standing alone, the job description certainly suggested that the gifted education coordinator should be classified as an administrator rather than a teacher.

The definition of what constituted a supervisor under Michigan law was more difficult to determine. The court discovered the term supervisor had not been defined by either the Michigan Labor Mediation Act or the Public Employment Relations Act. When such a void in the law exists, the court turns to federal labor law for guidance.

Under the Federal Labor Management Relations Act, the term supervisor was defined as:

any individual having authority in the interest of the employer, to hire, transfer, suspend, lay off, recall, promote, discharge, assign, reward, or discipline other employees . . . if . . . the exercise of such authority is not of a merely routine or clerical nature, but requires the use of independent judgment.

Federal courts had interpreted the above in such a manner that if an employee possessed one of the above duties, the employee fell into the supervisory category.

Applying this board definition, the Michigan court had no difficulty in finding that the coordinator's responsibilities were supervisory. The coordinator directed members of her staff and had a central role in the hiring process. Therefore, the appellate court concluded the position did not fall in the teaching category and the coordinator could not be represented by the local education association.

The second union case, *Colonial School Board v. Colonial Affiliate* (1982), concerned the scope of collective bargaining as it related to the gifted education curriculum.

A Delaware teacher's union sought an agreement with the school board as to what items could be the subject of collective bargaining. Among the items they wished to have included in the negotiations was "the development of programs for the educationally, socially, and emotionally disabled children as well as the educationally gifted students." The board rejected the union's proposal, subject to collective bargaining, but the local Chancery Court entered judgment for the union. The board then appealed the case to the Delaware Supreme Court.

Delaware's highest court reversed the ruling of the trial court. Chief Justice Herrmann found the Delaware statutes on collective bargaining controlling. Stated expressly in these statutes was that collective bargaining was to be limited to salaries, employee benefits, and working conditions. While the statutes did contain a clause that allowed the board and the negotiating representative of the union to agree to discuss "other matters," the court interpreted that provision of the statutes in a very narrow fashion. First, the court concluded that the previously mentioned statutory limitation, of the subject matter available for collective bargaining, controlled the "other matters" section of the collective bargaining portion of the code. Second, the other matters section was a narrow provision which applied only to discussion between the union representative and the board concerning matters that were of mutual interest between the two parties. It was not a provision which opened the door for all types of matters to be subject to collective bargaining.

Further complicating the union's position was that under the common law there was no right to bargain collectively. Following a widely held maxim in the law, the court held that any statute changing the common law had to be strictly construed. In this instance, the legislature had unambiguously carved out the subject matter available for collective bargaining between teachers and school boards.

Student transfers and bus rides, teacher certification, union representation and seniority questions, and other school policies will continue to spawn litigation as school administrators, teachers, parents, and students wrestle with problems in gifted education. As more states mandate the delivery of gifted education services, conflicts are certain to arise in these states concerning school policy on these and other equally perplexing questions. These few cases from several different jurisdictions provide an inadequate sample to gauge how certification, transfer, and seniority matters will be handled in future court decisions. But we can safely predict that the issues are so important that they will continually surface in the courts. The cases described above establish a foundation for the next series of legal battles.

Chapter 4
References

Colonial School Board v. Colonial Affiliate, NCCEA/DSEA/NEA 449 A. 2d 243 (Delaware Supreme Court 1982).

Davis v. Regional Board of School Trustees, 507 N.E. 2d 1352 (Illinois Appellate 5th District 1987).

Desmond v. Regional Board of School Trustees, 583 N.E. 2d 135 D (Illinois Appellate 3rd District 1989).

Green v. Jenkintown School District, 441 A. 2d 816 (Pennsylvania Commonwealth Court 1982).

Johnson v. Cassell, 387 S.E. 2d 553 (West Virginia 1989).

Michigan Education Association v. Clare-Gladwin Intermediate School District, 396 N.W. 2d 538 (Michigan Appellate 1986).

Renzulli, J. S. (1985). Are teachers of the gifted specialists? A landmark decision on employment practices in special education for the gifted. *Gifted Child Quarterly, 29,* 24-29.

Rosen v. Montgomery City Intermediate Unit No. 23, 495 A. 2d 217 (Pennsylvania Commonwealth Court 1985).

Rosenthal v. Orleans Parish School Board, 214 So. 2d 203 (Louisiana Appellate 1968).

Sands Point Academy v. Board of Education, 311 N.Y.S. 2d 588 (1970).

Shestach v. General Braddock Area School District, 437 A. 2d 1059 (Pennsylvania Commonwealth Court 1981).

Woodland Hills School v. Commonwealth Department of Education, 516 A. 2d 875 (Pennsylvania Commonwealth Court 1986).

—5—

Related Legal Issues and Gifted Youth

Divided into two major segments, accident and domestic relations cases, this chapter examines cases where the giftedness of the child is not the key issue being litigated, but is an ancillary factor in the court suit. For example, in an accident case where the gifted child is killed due to the defendant's negligence, should the parents of the gifted child receive a greater monetary award because the child was academically gifted and talented? A first reaction is that every child is of equal worth in the eyes of a parent. Yet, the gifted child may be capable in the future of providing greater aid to the parents, should the need arise. Or, in a divorce case where custody of the children is an issue, should the gifted child, all other things being equal, be placed with the parent who will allow the child to fully develop his or her educational abilities? These and similar questions are beginning to emerge in the courts.

Accident Cases and the Gifted

By discussing accidents involving gifted children, we are not suggesting that gifted children are more accident-prone. We know of no statistical study that would support this conclusion, yet gifted children often do have an insatiable intellectual curiosity that leads them into perilous undertakings. And, because of their participation in off-campus programs during vacation periods, they are often in situations where accidents can occur.

Consider, that between the years of 1984 and 1989, two students drowned during an outing arising from their participation in the College of Charleston Governor's School Mini-Session, one student was severely injured in a dormitory accident at the Mississippi Governor's School, and a fourth student was badly burned while performing a chemistry experiment at Murch Elementary School in Washington, DC. Relatives of one of the drowning victims sued the College of Charleston for two million dollars and the case was settled during trial immediately after a water safety expert testified on behalf of the plaintiffs.

The Murch School accident, which occurred during a summer program, also resulted in litigation, but the amount of damages awarded is sealed in the court records. The events surrounding this accident and the agony suffered by one of the injured children are described in *How It Feels to Fight for Your Life* by Jill Krementz (1989). In this work, Stewart Ugelow poignantly details the struggles he and his parents experienced following the accident.

To date, there is no record of any court suit filed in the Mississippi dormitory case. The lack of legal action may be because the state university that housed the program is immune from suit under the Mississippi sovereign immunity doctrine, one of the defenses available to some state dependents in accident cases. We hope that disseminating information about accident cases will make people more aware, and help prevent accidents in the future. This chapter will provide some insight as to the claims and defenses that can be raised in accident litigation involving gifted children.

Monetary Damages and Injuries to Gifted Children

The increased monetary recovery for the loss of a gifted child was addressed in *Gluckauf v. Pine Lake Beach Club*. In this 1963 New Jersey case, the issue relevant to this research was whether an award of $32,500 was an excessive award for the negligent death of a fifteen-year-old boy. The death stemmed from a swimming accident where the Pine Lake Beach Club was found negligent in providing safety personnel and equipment at the swimming facility.

On appeal, the defendant argued that the $32,500 award was excessive. Plaintiffs successfully countered this claim in two ways. First, they produced evidence indicating that the deceased did help his widowed mother by contributing to the maintenance of their residence and earning wages expected of a teenage boy. An important point in the area of gifted litigation was made when the court agreed that these contributions need not be set off by the cost of sending the child to college because the child was gifted and college expenses would be paid for by scholarships.

Second, the court held that the decedent had a bright future as a biochemist and would in all probability contribute to the support of his widowed mother. The mother had an income of $40–$50 per week at the time of the death and at age forty-nine had a life expectancy of twenty years. Given the decedent's high school IQ of 157 and his interest in science, the court did not feel that $32,500 was an excessive award to the mother. It is safe to say that in today's economic marketplace, the award would have been several times this amount.

Monetary Damages Based on Talents

Several civil cases suggest that courts take into account the giftedness and talents of children in injury cases. For example, a Louisiana appellate court upheld an award of $40,000 to the parents of a child killed in an automobile accident, the court pointing out the child was "a model, straight-A high school student, IQ 132 . . . who was attending college at the time of her death," *Wall v. American Employers Insurance Company* (1979). The Oklahoma Supreme Court overruled the state's industrial court finding that parents of an accidentally killed child suffered no pecuniary loss, noting that the deceased "was a talented musician and had a future in that field" and that "he was an exceptionally fine student," *Wallace v. State Industrial Court* (1965). A second case focusing on the talents of the deceased in regard to the award of monetary damages pointed out that a young girl was an honor student and a "gifted artist," *Terveer v. Baschnagel* (1982). Obversely, a New York trial court concluded that the award of $55,000 to the parents of a fifteen-year-

old who was killed when struck by an automobile was excessive
since there was no evidence that the boy had any "specific ambition
in life" or "that he had any area in which he was especially talented,"
Wishart v. Andress (1974).

Injury in a Resident Program

An illustration of how *not* to handle an injury occurring at a
residence program is contained in *Martinez v. Western Carolina
University* (1980). A detailed presentation of the facts is necessary
to appreciate the significance of the case.

At the time of the accident, J. Michael Martinez was a fourteen-
year-old student enrolled in the Western Carolina University summer program for gifted children. Early one Saturday, while running
in the dormitory, Michael slipped on a puddle of water in a hallway,
severely injuring his ankle. When ice and rest did not ameliorate
his discomfort, he asked his counselor to take him to the campus
infirmary. The counselor replied that since it was the housemother's
responsibility to obtain medical care for the students, Michael
should contact her instead. Michael was unable to locate the housemother until 8 P.M., and she told the plaintiff that she would take
him to the infirmary the next day.

The examining doctor's diagnosis of the swollen ankle was that
Michael had suffered an Achilles sprain. During a conversation with
his mother on the following Tuesday, Michael told his mother about
the accident and she asked to speak to the counselor. The counselor
promised to see that Michael was taken to the infirmary the next
day. At 5 P.M. the next day when his mother called, Michael informed
her that he had not seen a physician. A conversation with the housemother brought a promise to take Michael to the infirmary that
evening. This promise was kept, although there was no doctor on
duty after 6 P.M., and the nurse on duty reiterated that the injury
was a sprain.

On July 7, five days after the accident, Michael and his fellow
students participated in a hike through Joyce Kilmer National Park.
Michael, using a stick and a cane and taking shortcuts, finished the
hike, but evidently this exercise aggravated the injury. On July 8,

his mother was informed that Michael had a ruptured Achilles tendon and needed to be excused from the program. His mother rented a plane and the plaintiff was flown to Florence, North Carolina where surgery was performed the next day. Testimony in the case indicated that although the surgery was more extensive because of the delay in medical treatment, Michael would suffer no long term effects, other than perhaps some additional scarring, because of the postponement of proper medical care. However, there is some language in the court's opinion that at one time during the proceedings, Michael's entire foot was in jeopardy.

Under North Carolina State Tort Claims Act, the plaintiff's claim had to be filed before the North Carolina Industrial Commission. Hearing the case alone, the deputy commissioner awarded the plaintiff $13,000 for pain and suffering and permanent scarring. Unfortunately, the full commission reversed the deputy commissioner's decision and abolished the award.

The court of appeals, however, disagreed with the full commissions' decision. Noting that the commission had glossed over the claims of negligence against university staff personnel, the appeals court sent the case back to the industrial commission so that they could focus on the negligence issue. At this point, the record of the case ends, but the facts of the case appear to dictate the outcome. It is probably safe to say that if a director of a residence program was more responsive to the injured student initially, liability would be reduced.

Off-Campus Injuries

Cases from Louisiana, *Powell v. Orleans Parish Schools* (1978), and California, *Bozanich v. Kenney* (1970), depict the problems that can arise when bright and talented students participate in special events or programs off campus. Both cases illustrate how an activity slated to benefit the child can become life threatening despite the best intentions of parents, teachers, and school administrators.

David Powell Jr. was a member of his Orleans Parish high school band which was participating in a band festival in Galveston, Texas. David, according to testimony provided at the trial by his father, was a good, obedient, and gifted boy. The band trip, according to his father, was a reward for his past accomplishments.

Shortly after arriving at Galveston, in fact even before the check-in process at the motel had been completed, several band members decided to take a dip in the pool. David joined the swimmers, and although he could not swim, inexplicably dove into the water off the diving board located at the deep end of the pool. Discovered lying at the bottom of the pool, he was pulled from the pool and given artificial respiration. Tragically, all efforts to revive him failed.

Several issues raised in the negligence suit brought by the father against the Orleans Parish School Board are of interest. The first centered on the question of whether there was an adequate number of chaperons present on the trip and whether they were negligent in supervising the swimmers. Both the trial court and the appeals court concluded that the evidence indicated the supervision was adequate at the pool. It was also detrimental to the father's argument that he had signed a permission slip for his son to go swimming. No conditions were placed on the permission and the father did not notify school authorities that his son could not swim. The Louisiana appeals court concluded that the facts of the case prohibited a negligence action and sustained the trial court's dismissal of the suit. The appeals court also charged the parent with the cost of bringing the appeal. While each side would still pay for their attorney's fees, the plaintiff would have to pay the incidental costs such as court reporting fees, copying costs, etc.

The 1970 California Supreme Court case, although somewhat dated from the perspective of the legal principle involved, provides an example of how easily lawsuits can arise. Two California high school classmates, Carey Bozanich and Terence Kenney, were selected to participate in a Spanish class for gifted students taught at the University of Southern California. After reviewing several transportation options, the students and their parents agreed that the best choice was for Terence and Carey to drive the ten miles to the university in Terence's newly acquired Sunbeam automobile. Carey's contribution to the transportation expenses would be to pay the $8.75 university parking fee.

All went well until approximately the third week of the gifted program. At that time, while commuting either to or from the program, the Sunbeam, traveling at a high rate of speed, crossed the centerline and was involved in an accident. Carey sued Terence alleging her personal injuries were caused by the negligent driving. As the Supreme Court's opinion explains, the defense came close to admitting negligence in the trial court. What was at issue was whether Terence was protected from suit by California's guest passenger statute.

Guest passenger statutes were introduced in some states to protect drivers from liability when they provided rides to friends, neighbors, etc. State legislatures thought that a voluntary act of kindness should not result in a driver placing his or her assets at risk should the automobile be involved in an accident and the "guest" passenger injured. Today, the need for such statutes has been largely negated through the holding of liability insurance. That is, everyone realizes that although the driver of the automobile is the named plaintiff, the insurance contract requires the company to defend and pay a judgment to the limits of the policy. Therefore, guest passenger laws, like the governmental and parental immunity doctrines, have generally gone by the wayside.

In this case, the specific issue was the judge's jury instruction concerning the application of the guest passenger statute in this case. Of great importance was whether the judge's instruction that the jury had to find the $8.75 was the main motivating factor in Terence's tendering a ride to Carey. If the $8.75 was not the influential reason for sharing transportation, the judge instructed the jury that Carey would be considered a guest and the guest passenger statute would prevent her from recovering damages. Carey lost her case at trial, but the California Supreme Court found the jury instruction was prejudicial and sent the case back to the lower court to reexamine the application of the guest passenger statute, particularly given the educational purpose of the trips.

The significance of this rather minor case is that it highlights what may go wrong in a seemingly harmless travel arrangement. Throughout the country, travel to and from off-campus gifted programs is commonplace, which provides an opportunity for all types of litigation. In many instances students share rides on both a paid and unpaid basis. When transportation to such a program is provided on a regular basis by a private party, parents involved in these situations should know such items as the applicability of any limitation on recovery such as a guest passenger statute, the insurance coverage of the provider of the transportation, the presence of any waivers of liability, etc. Parents then can better evaluate the public and private options for travel to the gifted program. Interestingly, in the *Bozanich* case, the parents originally rejected public bus transportation to the Spanish program as being too expensive.

Injuries Related to Products

Patrick v. Perfect Parts Company (1974) and *Dieringer v. Plain Township* (no reported written opinion) have nothing to do specifically with gifted education programs. Rather, they illustrate the problems that can arise when dealing with intellectually gifted children. They are presented here, not because they provide any important insights into litigation involving gifted children, but with the hope that their discussion will in some way prevent similar tragedies in the future.

Tom Patrick was a seven-year-old child at the time of the accident and, according to the Missouri Supreme Court opinion, an "exceptionally bright student" and, we can assume from his actions, an intellectually curious child as well. Tom, his sister (age ten) and a friend (age twelve) decided they would create gun powder by mixing sulfur, charcoal, and sodium nitrate. This experiment, carried out behind Tom's garage, was somewhat successful as the children were able to burn a hole through a tin bowl and produce sufficient smoke to bring Tom's mother rushing to the scene. The project was classified as only somewhat successful as the chemicals were thrown away and the youngest incipient scientist received a spanking.

Not to be deterred, the next few days found the young scientists back at work with their chemicals, which this time consisted of denatured alcohol and some magnesium ribbon. During the proceedings, Tom accidentally spilled alcohol on his clothing and when a match was lit, his clothing caught fire and he was severely burned on his legs and the right and front side of his body.

Tom's father, suing in behalf of his child, brought a products liability suit against the makers of the alcohol. His contention was that the failure of the manufacturer to designate, on the label of the bottle, the flammability of denatured alcohol constituted negligence on behalf of the manufacturer. Although the Patricks won their case before a jury, the trial judge overturned the jury's verdict and decided the case in favor of the manufacturer. Unfortunately for Tom, the intermediate court of appeals, and the Missouri Supreme Court, agreed with the judge. All three levels of judges concluded that the evidence submitted at trial indicated "this bright youngster knew the burning propensities of denatured alcohol . . and was in possession of all the information an adequate warning could have afforded." Evidently, however, Tom was not concerned enough about the flammability of the product to prevent his serious injury.

If the *Patrick* case illustrates the curiosity of the bright child, *Dieringer* depicts the instance where intellectually gifted children are often asked to perform tasks beyond their capabilities. Parents and teachers become so used to treating them as intellectually mature that physical and awareness limitations of the young are forgotten. Such was the case in the tragic death of Laura Dieringer.

Laura was an exemplary student at Warstler Elementary School. A member of Mensa, she was often selected, as a reward for her good school work, to perform certain tasks for the teacher. One day in the fall of 1984, when the seven-year-old was requested to bring the video cart into the regular classroom, the television on top of the cart toppled off, crushing the back of her head. Obviously, a taller and more physically mature person would not have been prone to such serious injury.

A suit brought by the Dieringers against the school district was lost at trial and they decided not to pursue the litigation through the appellate courts. Instead, Jim and Kathy Dieringer, Laura's parents, have used her tragic death to try to make other parents aware of the dangers when teachers ask students to perform tasks, or use equipment, that places the children at risk. Writing in an open letter to parents of gifted children in *Gifted Child Monthly* (1985), Jim and Kathy point out that gifted children often have an acute sense of responsibility to perform tasks requested by educators. And as Professor James Delisle (1985) has discussed, it is usually the good and model student, and often the gifted child, who gets caught in the gap between "physical agility and mental acuity."

Yesterday's American jurisprudence did not place great monetary value on the death of, or injury to, a child. Within the past few years, courts have started awarding million dollar verdicts to parents of children who have been severely injured or killed. There is no doubt that skilled plaintiff lawyers will attempt to increase monetary awards by placing into evidence the intellectual or artistic capabilities of the accident victim.

Domestic Relations Cases and the Gifted

We were surprised by the number of child custody and child support cases where the giftedness of the child became an issue. This giftedness issue often arose in divorce cases when the judge was faced with the decision of which parent should receive physical custody of the child. While there are many factors that judges weigh in determining the custodial parent such as the age, gender, and the best interest of the child, the opportunity for the child to participate in a gifted education program or attend a private school has become a specific issue in several cases. The cases described below provide a representative sampling of domestic relations cases where the giftedness of the child became an issue in the divorce proceedings.

Child Support

Before examining a representative sample of the custody cases, a collateral issue arising in the domestic relations case law needs to be mentioned. It concerns the financial requirement needed to maintain a gifted child. Judges usually assess the noncustodial parent with child support payments that allow the child to continue the standard of living in place at the time of the separation. Because judges maintain continuing jurisdiction over these cases, when there is a significant change in the child's needs, for example, if the child's best interest would be met by attending a private school, the court can raise or lower child support payments as circumstances warrant.

An example of the need for a change in the level of financial support is illustrated in the 1982 Louisiana case, *Castille v. Buck*. In that case, the trial court ordered the noncustodial father to pay $500 per month child support and the father appealed. Both parents were in the education profession and earned approximately the same salary.

The appellate court found the trial court award excessive and reduced the father's payment to $400 per month. Finding that both parents had a duty to support the ten-year-old child, the appellate court concluded that the trial court's acceptance of the mother's determination of the financial needs of the child was erroneous. But what is important here is that the appellate court noted that the child was gifted and on a waiting list of a private school. However, the child was not attending the private school at the time of the divorce and therefore the cost of attendance could not be taken into account. However, the appellate court's recognition of the child's possible future needs, i.e., the opportunity to attend the private school, would provide a firm foundation for a request for a child support increase when the child did gain entrance to the private school.

The amount of financial support required of a noncustodial parent was also at issue in the 1980 *Rohn v. Thuma* case. In this Indiana case, the question was whether a divorce decree, which stated that the father was "to provide each child with a four year undergraduate college education," required the father to pay tuition and expenses at a prestigious private university. Both the sons were gifted and had graduated at the top of their high school class. One child requested funds to attend the University of Chicago, while the other child wished to attend Vassar. The Indiana Court of Appeals held that the father only had to provide funds sufficient to attend a local public state university.

Troubling the appellate court was the ambiguity of the provision requiring the father to provide a university education for his sons. The mother interpreted the provision as meaning any university while the father obviously believed he had met the requirements of the decree by tendering monies allowing the children to attend a state supported university. In this particular case, the father, the court concluded, could afford the expense of sending the children to the private schools, but the ambiguity of the provision in question did not sustain the argument that the father had violated the divorce decree. Therefore, on this issue the appellate court agreed with the trial court that the father could not be held in contempt of court.

The opinion is helpful to persons interested in the law relating to education of the gifted in two ways. First, the opinion cites a list of cases where state courts have decided such ambiguous provisions in a similar fashion. It thus provides a good summary of the rule of law used in construing clauses in a divorce decree where the cost of a college education is incorporated in the decree. The Indiana court followed the majority rule in its decision as most state courts have held that the paying parent must only provide the costs of a public school education.

Second, the court, in a footnote, provided some sage advice to parents and laywers drafting college degree provisions in divorce decrees. In footnote one, the court advised:

We might note that in drafting any such agreement or proposed support entry, counsel for the parties should be cognizant of the children's long range educational needs and desires and the costs thereof regardless of the ages of the children at the date of dissolution and should provide accordingly with some degree of specificity.

The advice for parents is, despite the fact that the child might only be in the third grade, if the child indicates intellectual promise, the decree should be worded in a way which will allow the child to develop his or her academic talents. For example, the clause could read that the paying parent would provide a university education for the child to the university of the child's choice provided that the paying parent could afford the cost. The provision should also be specific as to whether the costs included tuition, travel, books, food, housing, and clothes. Usually the greater the specificity in drafting divorce decrees, the less litigation is needed down the road. If the decree is properly worded, the only determination left to the court would be the paying parent's capacity to provide the required funds.

Modification in child support was also at issue in *Howard v. Howard*. In this 1974 case, an Alabama trial judge increased the child support sufficiently to allow the custodial mother to place two children in a private school. Noting that the children had been designated "exceptional" and the oldest child was attending a gifted program in the public school system, the judge accepted the mother's argument that the best interest of the children demanded that they be placed in a private school. In the private school, the mother testified, the children would have more individual attention and have greater access to art and music programs. The father, a physician, was ordered to increase the child support to $700 per month to cover the increased private school tuition. In this case, it is clear from the opinion that the giftedness of the children played an important role in the judge's decision.

A 1989 Michigan case, *Adkins v. Adkins*, also recognizes that "special circumstances" might dictate that child support payments continue beyond age eighteen, even when the child is still in secondary school rather than a university. Although *Adkins* concerns a child who had a poor school record and thus was still in the tenth grade at age eighteen, the Michigan Court of Appeals defined special circumstances as follows:

1. the child's aptitude and motivation to achieve at an institution of higher education;
2. likelihood of child's good-faith performance;
3. whether the child is handicapped and requires special training;
4. costs of the child's future education program;
5. whether the child is particularly gifted.

Adkins contributes to the case law concerning gifted children in that the educationally gifted are included in the definition of "special circumstances." While the case was decided by a state court and is only applicable as a precedent in Michigan, the case could be cited by lawyers in other states as a precedent that their state should adopt in child support litigation.

Custody Cases

Turning to the sample of child custody cases, it isequally clear that a child's "giftedness" is often taken into account by trial judges in awarding custody. In *Goldman v. Logue* (1984), a Louisiana appellate court upheld a trial judge's decision that while both appeared to be caring parents, the nine-year-old gifted child had progressed intellectually in the sole custody of the father. Citing this finding and the parents' ongoing divisiveness regarding the child's well being, the judge refused to grant the mother's request that she be awarded joint custody. Interestingly, the judge granted sole custody to the father despite the Louisiana statutory presumption that parents should be awarded joint custody of their offspring.

An Alabama appellate court in *Altieri v. Altieri* (1988) also refused to change the original custody award when the trial judge had placed an eleven-year-old girl with her father. Testimony indicated that the child had made very good grades while living with her father and was participating in her school's gifted education program. Although the divorce had been awarded partially on the basis of the father's adultery, the trial and appellate courts still concluded it was in the best interest of the girl to remain with her father. While other factors entered into this finding, the intellectual development of the child appears to have played a key role in the decision of the trial and the appellate courts.

For a representative sample, we need to include a case where the opportunity to attend a gifted school did not help persuade a judge to modify custody. In *Meneou v. Meneou* (1987), an Indiana Court of Appeals refused to modify a joint legal custody award to a sole custody award to the mother. Originally, the father had been awarded physical custody with joint legal custody being awarded to both parents. The mother had requested a modification in an Indiana trial court as she had remarried and moved to Louisville, Kentucky which had a gifted education program. Because the school-age child had been identified as an exceptional learner, she argued that he could best be served educationally by living with her and attending the Louisville gifted education program. However, the court did not accept her argument. Instead, the court awarded sole custody to the father based on the testimony of a psychiatrist that it would be in the best interest of the children to reside permanently at one location. Under the previous joint legal custody arrangement, the children had been regularly transferred between the two locations. Under the new award, which was upheld by the appellate court, the father was given sole custody with liberal visitation to be granted to the mother. The appellate court's opinion did not consider educational opportunities for the gifted child in the father's school district.

Summary

As stated at the outset, there are no data which support the idea that gifted and talented children are more prone to accidents than other children. However, they do find themselves in situations where their intellectual curiosity, or the gap between their intellectual ability and their physical ability, or their participation in special gifted programs, places them at risk. It is the responsibility of parents, teachers, and school administrators to make certain those risks are minimized so that tragic injuries and deaths do not occur.

And with the awareness of competition in today's job market, judges will increasingly consider educational opportunities as a factor in child support and custody decisions. Given the standard of making decisions in the best interest of the child, judges will have to weigh opportunities for the child to develop his or her intellectual abilities. While such a consideration will remain just one of the factors in the formula, the increasing identification of gifted children, and the proliferation of gifted programs, will result in more judges taking the giftedness of the child into account during custody and support litigation. After all, it is the "best interest" of the child that is at stake and the giftedness factor needs to be inserted in the custody and support equation.

Chapter 5
References

Adkins v. Adkins, 448 N.W. 2d 741 (Michigan Appellate 1989).

Altieri v. Altieri, 528 So. 2d 861 (Alabama Civil Appellate 1988).

Bozanich v. Kenney, 91 Cal. Rptr. 286, 477 P. 2d142 (1970).

Castille v. Buck, 411 So. 2d 1156 (Louisiana Appellate 1982).

Delisle, J. R. (1985). Saying no for safey's sake. *Gifted Child Monthly,* 6(3) 1-3. Also see letter to parents from Jim and Kathy Dieringer following the Delisle article.

Dieringer v. Plain Township (No reported opinion). Information concerning this case was received from communication with Jim and Kathy Dieringer.

Gluckauf v. Pine Lake Beach Club, 187 A. 2d 357 (New Jersey 1963).

Goldman v. Logue, 461 So. 2d 469 (Louisiana Appellate 5th Circuit 1984).

Howard v. Howard, 301 So. 2d 191 (Alabama 1974).

Krementz, J. (Ed.). (1989). *How it feels to fight for your life.* Boston: Little, Brown and Company.

Martinez v. Western Carolina University, 271 S.E. 2d 91 (North Carolina Appellate 1980).

Meneou v. Meneou, 503 N.E. 2d 902 (Indiana Appellate 1987).

Patrick v. Perfect Parts Co., 515 S.W. 554 (Missouri 1974).

Powell v. Orleans Parish School Board, 354 So. 2d 229 (Louisiana Appellate 1978).

Rohn v. Thuma, 408 N.E. 2d 578 (Indiana Appellate 1980).

Terveer v. Baschnagel, 445 N.E. 2d 264 (Ohio Appellate 1982).

Wall v. American Employers Insurance, 377 So. 2d 369 (Louisiana Appellate 1980).

Wallace v. State Industrial Court, 406 P. 2d 488 (Oklahoma 1965).

Wishart v. Andress, 361 N.Y.S. 2d 791 (1974).

—6—

Mediation and Gifted Education

Every year, many local school districts initiate new programs for the gifted. One by one, states are joining the ranks of those in which gifted education has been made mandatory. Parents and other advocacy groups for the gifted are becoming better informed about what is going on elsewhere and what is feasible locally in gifted education; they are becoming more vocal and impatient as they exert influence on local school boards and school personnel. Recent developments in the field of gifted education are likely to be followed by an increasing number of instances in which school board members, school administrators, directors, coordinators of programs for the gifted, and parents of bright children will need help in resolving conflicts and settling issues.

Any parent or group who is displeased with a decision or wishes to see changes made in school policies or programs should first marshal the relevant facts, laws, policies and procedures; formulate in clear terms any written proposal to be presented, and then follow proper channels in seeking discussions of the matter at hand with appropriate school authorities — teacher, principal, gifted and talented coordinator, or curriculum specialist. Individuals and groups improve the chances of negotiating successfully and serving their interests well if, when making a proposal, they remember that school officials and board members are continuously receiving conflicting recommendations. Consider for a moment the plight of the superintendent and school board members who are under pressure from many of the most ardent sports enthusiasts of the community for increased emphasis on competitive athletics vis-a-vis other vocal patrons who are pressing for higher academic standards.

We repeat: The best way for interested parties to bring about change in the school is to prepare a well-reasoned position statement which takes into account what is reasonable and feasible, then to abide by current policies and procedures in presenting that case through established channels. Only after sincere attempts to pursue informal negotiations have failed, should determined advocates for change turn to mediation as an approach to conflict resolution.

Even prior to informal negotiations or before beginning the mediation process, the parties in a dispute should document their activities. A record of telephone calls, personal visits, and letters written can be as essential to the case as the more substantive, well-reasoned argument mentioned above. Records become doubly important to all parties in the event satisfactory solutions are not achieved and a decision is made to turn to mediation as the next alternative to conflict resolution in a nonadversarial manner.

Mediation is a new procedure in education and little has been written about it. The publications of two national associations, *The Neighborhood Justice System* and the *National Association of State Directors of Special Education*, both written in 1982, have been helpful resources. The work of Ekstrand and Edmister written in 1984 has also contributed to the information presented in this chapter.

Some state educational agencies have developed guidelines for mediation; others have not. All states need to have a well-developed document on mediation, which then should be disseminated to local districts. This could be done through legislative enactment or by the state department of education issuing regulations under an appropriate grant of power. State consultants in gifted education will have the information on mediation for their state (Appendix F). For readers in the states without mediation, the suggestions provided in Chapter 7 for the establishment of due process will be helpful.

The state department of education, or another state agency, is usually responsible for selecting, training, and appointing mediators. The state agency also supervises the mediation process and the conduct of mediators. The mediation agreement should be reviewed by the state education agency to determine if all components are in compliance with policies and laws both at the state and federal levels.

Further, there should be a professional staff person appointed to coordinate all of the mediation activities. This person will be responsible for appointing mediators, acting as an information resource on mediation, updating the mediators on best practices, and maintaining confidential files on all mediation agreements. The state consultant in gifted education should review all the mediation agreements on an annual basis to determine commonalities, if any, for the purpose of initiating and/or revising appropriate regulations and/or policies and procedures.

The Mediation Process

Mediation is a process by which disputes are resolved in an informal manner. From an educational vantage point, the informality and nonadversarial features of this approach to conflict resolution give mediation distinct advantages over due process and litigation. Mediation offers the best chance that amiable and cooperative working relationships will accompany and follow the reaching of agreements. Another consideration which favors mediation is that this process requires much less money and time than do the alternatives. Courts do not enter the picture, and thus legal counsel is neither required nor recommended. Decisions or agreements are usually reached in a few days or a week or two after the request for a mediation meeting.

The major difference between mediation and negotiation within the school district is that mediation involves the services of a disinterested person, usually from outside the district, who is specially trained to help resolve conflict in an informal setting.

Mediator Qualifications

The person selected as a mediator in some states may be an employee of a public school system, state department of education, a college or university, another community agency or may be from the private sector. In other states, the person must be from a general pool of mediators employed by the state to settle a variety of disputes, with education being one of them.

A mediator who is called upon to help resolve local conflicts which arise in the area of gifted education must know the state and federal laws and regulations related to the issue to be mediated, as well as any case law. The person should have a basic understanding of the local policies and procedures, and be aware of the programs and services available within the school district. Acquaintance with the procedures and assessment instruments used in the identification and evaluation of the gifted is helpful as is an understanding of the unique characteristics and needs of the gifted.

The personal qualities of the mediator are of major importance. The ability to relate well to both parties involved is of prime concern, as are good communication skills, both verbal and nonverbal. The mediator must know how to facilitate group discussion; he or she should be especially skillful at identifying issues, delineating the various positions with reference to them, and presenting workable alternative solutions for consideration. The mediator should be adept at dealing with controversy in a nonthreatening and nonargumentative manner and able to effectively manage the group process under conditions which can at times become very stressful. The mediator must be well-versed in group dynamics and senstive to the feelings of others but he or she must maintain objectivity while exercising good judgment.

Because they are responsible for writing an acceptable agreement reached as a result of the mediation process, mediators need good writing skills. The agreement must be written in such a way so that it is readable and understandable to all parties involved.

The mediator's professional and personal qualities must indicate to all parties that disagreement will be handled in an impartial manner and that confidentiality will be maintained. Mediators are professionally trained to perform their duties; such training is usually the responsibility of the state.

Setting Up a Mediation Meeting

The time, place, and date for the mediation meeting will be mutually established and the mediator should confirm, in writing, the information to the parents and others directly concerned. The facility for the meeting needs to be conducive to positive interactions; the room should be large enough to accommodate the participants and should be well lighted and ventilated to be comfortable. The place selected, usually within the school district, must provide privacy and ensure freedom from such distractions as interruptions and disruptive noises. A separate room should be accessible for the mediator to meet with each party individually. A recorder or secretary should be present. Access to a typewriter and photocopying machine would be desirable. All records and other data and materials needed in the session should be available. Refreshments and provisions for lunch, if needed, should be arranged.

The mediator should let everyone know that mediation sessions usually last only a short period of time. Few will last as long as a day, with the majority conducted within a three- to five-hour time period. No limitation should be imposed, however, as all parties should have as much time as needed. There may be a reason to conduct the mediation session over several days, and this should be allowed; parties must have ample time to consider all the possibilities for reaching agreement.

Mediation Session Confirmation Letter to Parents

Date
Parents' Names
Address
City, State, Zip Code

Dear (Parents' Names):

During our telephone conversation of (Date), it was mutually agreed that a mediation session would take place on (Date), (Time), at (Building and Address). Mediation is a flexible and informal way of resolving issues through understanding and compromise of different points of view. The mediation process allows both parties to present their positions with the purpose of seeking a solution. Mediation does not require the canceling of the due process hearing, if one has been requested.

Most mediation sessions take from two to six hours. You are asked to remain the entire session, so please plan accordingly. Sometimes sessions may need to be extended or rescheduled. Please bring all information needed for the session.

Persons with knowledge of your child or having information concerning your child in regard to the issue may accompany you. It is my understanding at this time that the following persons will be with you:

      (Name)   (Title)
      (Name)   (Title)

Additional persons may also accompany you, if you wish.

The following persons will attend the session from (Name) school district:

      (Name)   (Title)
      (Name)   (Title)

If you have concerns regarding the above information, or if further assistance is needed, please contact me.

Sincerely,

Name and Title (Mediator)

Mediation Session Notice to School District Personnel

(Date)

TO: (List all district personnel by name and title)

FROM: Name and Title (Mediator)

RE: Mediation session involving (Child's Name)

Your attendance is requested at a mediation session to be held on (Date), (Time), at (Building and Location).

The (Name) school district and the parents (Names) have agreed to a mediation meeting. Mediation is a flexible and informal way of resolving issues through understanding and compromise of different points of view. The mediation process allows both parties to present their positions with the purpose of seeking a solution. Mediation does not require the canceling of the due process hearing (if one is allowable and has been requested).

Most mediation sessions take from two to six hours. You are asked to remain the entire session, so please plan accordingly. Sometimes sessions may need to be extended or rescheduled. Please bring all information needed for the session.

If you have any questions, please contact me.

Who Participates in the Mediation Session?

The persons involved in the session will vary depending on the purpose of the mediation. Only those persons necessary for the discussion of the issues relevant to the case should be present. Those representing the school system may include, but not be limited to, school principal, the director of the gifted program, the teacher of the gifted and/or the regular classroom teacher responsible for the instructional program of the student, curriculum specialist, school psychologist, or a social worker. One of the school district participants should be a person with the authority to speak for the district and implement decisions and agreements reached.

Parents should use discretion and take maturity into account in deciding whether the child or children under consideration should be included in the session. In making such a decision, parents must give serious attention to the nature and substance of the discussions which are likely to occur and the possible effects on the student's well-being and self-concept.

For assistance in presenting a good case, parents should feel free to bring to the session two or three persons who might serve as advocates for gifted education or as outside evaluators. Such persons should be selected for their knowledge of facts relevant to the case. Both parties may have a legal advisor if they so choose, but this is usually neither necessary nor desirable. The mediator should caution both the school district and the parents about having too many people present, reminding them that a smaller group will facilitate communication.

The Parents' Role

The parents or the guardian should attend the meeting in good faith, with a positive outlook, and with full intention of reaching an agreement. The entire day should be set aside for the meeting, although sessions usually last only a few hours. The parents have the responsibility for gathering and understanding the facts which they want to present in a straightforward and objective manner. These may include laws, rules and regulations of the local district and the state department of education, test scores, and other performance-based information on the child. Parents should be active in the discussion, asking questions and stating their views clearly. Working through the mediator, parents should, at appropriate times, help provide opportunities for any persons they may have invited to the session to make contributions to the discussions.

When the parents meet separately with the mediator, they should be prepared to offer viable alternative solutions. Depending on the issue, alternatives may include early admission, an IEP, grade skipping, or acceleration in a specific academic area. They must accept the mediator not as a person whose role is to settle the dispute, but one who will assist in the solution seeking process.

When consensus is reached, the parent must carefully read the agreement, ask for clarification if necessary, and sign it with a commitment to follow the decisions set forth. If it seems impossible to reach an agreement, the parents should then seek other courses of action available to them, such as due process or the courts.

The School District's Role

Representatives of the school district should also attend the mediation session in good faith and with the intention of reaching an agreement. A day should be scheduled for the meeting, although usually only a few hours are necessary. As indicated earlier, there should be a representative from the school empowered with the authority to act on behalf of the district. The authorization must be established before the mediation session begins. The representatives of the school district should be active in the discussion and in drafting the mediation agreement. They should state the facts and all relevant information in a straightforward and objective way. Solutions to the dispute should be offered when meeting separately with the mediator. Especially important will be the active participation of the representative who has the knowledge and the authority to guarantee that every point of the mediation agreement will be met. For example, the curriculum specialist will know the scope of academic course offerings. The principal will know the class schedule and any variations, which could provide for flexibility. The fee and expenses of a mediator are normally paid by the school district or by the state education agency.

Preparing for the Mediation Session

Thorough preparation for the mediation meeting is essential for everyone involved — the mediator as well as the school district and the parents.

The mediator must have full knowledge of the facts. These may be gathered from school records and all other documents relevant to the case, including notes of previous meetings. The parents will also have information and facts which will be helpful to the mediator. The issues must be clearly identified, and the mediator should know the positions of the parties involved. The results of a mediation session will be heavily influenced by the extent to which the mediator is prepared to provide ample consideration of alternative solutions, each of which has a chance of attracting support and agreement.

The school district's representative, the parents, and others representing both parents and the school need access to, and should be knowledgeable about, the records of the child and other documents bearing on the dispute.

Parents should seek the meaning of the educational terms needing definition. They should also have in writing — and have read — the policies and regulations of the school district, those of the state department of education, and other relevant agencies. (Copies of state laws are available from the office of the attorney general or the superintendent of public instruction.) Information on any previous meetings on the topic with school personnel, including dates, times, and names of those present, should be available.

Both parties need to be afforded an opportunity to offer solutions to the dispute.

Mediation Session

The mediator sets the tone of the meeting. The session is held between individuals who have a dispute to settle. The meeting is not as formal as a due process hearing, but is more formal than a typical school conference.

As participants arrive for the session, the mediator will greet and get acquainted with each individual and make sure that all of the participants know each other by name, position or title and reason for participation. As the time approaches for the meeting to begin and with participants seated in a circle or around a table to facilitate communication, the mediator should identify each participant by name and position. Brief words of welcome should be followed immediately by a clear and concise statement of the purpose of the session. Then the mediator will explain his or her role with emphasis on the major responsibilities: listening attentively, posing questions, providing technical assistance, presenting alternatives, and maintaining an impartial posture throughout the deliberations. The mediator should stress the importance of confidentiality if the purpose of the meeting is to be well served. The goal of working toward an amiable, mutually acceptable agreement should be made apparent to all.

After offering a very brief overview of prior efforts to resolve the issue at hand, the mediator should ask whomever requested the session to speak first. That person should then present without interruption the position he or she would like the other participants to consider. A spokesperson for the second party can then be called upon to present in similar fashion the position of that party. If by good fortune there are points of agreement in the two position statements, the mediator should call attention to and emphasize these elements of concurrence as the meeting is opened for discussion. At this point each participant is afforded an opportunity to raise questions, make comments, offer suggestions, present additional information or otherwise contribute and ensure thorough consideration of the issue or issues which brought the group together.

The mediator's skills as a discussion leader are especially important to the success of the mediation session. Throughout the lively discussions which generally ensue, the mediator should provide ample opportunities for all relevant information to be presented and for all points of view to find expression. All participants must be heard, and it's the mediator's job to ensure that the time made available to more timid participants will be equitable to that utilized by the bold.

From the beginning and throughout the session, the mediator will be looking for and taking note of points of agreement and statements of position afforded support by both parties. During the latter part of the session, the search for consensus should receive increased emphasis as the mediator tests ideas and points of view which might be included in a summary and concluding statement.

For example, both parties might agree on an accelerated reading program or an IEP to include more enrichment activities in science. In the conclusion there will be the order of general support which will set the stage for the preparation of written terms of agreement positively endorsed by both parties.

Sample Mediation Agreement Outline

Date of Mediation Session:

Mediator:

Student's Name:

Student's School:

Parents' Name:

Address:

Name of School District:

Person in attendance with the parents:

>   Name, Title
>   Name, Title

Persons in attendance with the school district:

>   Name, Title
>   Name, Title

Summary of Issues:

Recommendations:
1.
2.
3.

Effective date to ending date: _____

Parents' Signatures: _____

_____

Signature of School District Personnel responsible for Authorizing and Monitoring: _____

Mediator's Signature: _____

Use of the Caucus in the Mediation Process

Caucusing, or meeting privately with each party, can be very effective in moving toward conflict resolution. The mediator should present this approach as an option available to him or her and to both parties at any time after the two parties have presented their case. Judicious use of the caucus will be up to the mediator, but either party should feel free to request and be granted time for a caucus with the mediator at any time the progress and tone of the deliberations suggest that such a private meeting would be helpful in reaching agreement. The skillful mediator will be especially adept at timing the use of the caucus with the member of one party and then with the other to enhance the chances of ultimate agreement.

Some of the many circumstances which can and do arise to suggest the need for caucuses with the two parties are as follows:

1. One or both parties begin to express such strong feelings and so much hostility is developing that progress toward agreement may be impeded or reversed.

2. The need to move beyond an impasse becomes apparent.

3. Members of one or both parties become unduly reluctant to express their feelings, state their position clearly, or indicate the extent of agreement or disagreement with the opposition in the presence of members of the opposing party.

4. The mediator senses that some of the participants need time and privacy to save face, cool off and relieve tension, or to seek clarification and explore options with colleagues.

5. Substantial progress toward agreement is being made, but an aggressive member of one party or the other is blocking further movement.

6. Progress has been such that the mediator senses that the time has come for him or her to explore, in private with each party, the major points to be included in a written agreement which would gain the concurrence and support of both parties.

Clearly, the caucus, if properly employed, serves as much more than a last resort to which the mediator or opposing parties turn in instances of impasse. The caucus provides the mediator with an excellent opportunity to gain and maintain rapport with, and the respect and confidence of, both parties and convince both of the impartiality and confidentiality of the proceedings. Both parties in a conflict become intimately and directly involved in the deliberations; the caucus helps both enjoy the assurance that they participated fully in the session or sessions which culminated in a written agreement. They are more likely to feel that this agreement not only merits their signatures willingly affixed but deserves their full and enthusiastic support.

In the event that a single session does not lead to general consensus and agreement on resolution of the original points of contention, the mediator's responsibility becomes that of encouraging the two parties to join in the formulation of plans for a subsequent meeting or meetings. Typically, a first session, even though agreement may not be achieved, should enable both parties to prepare for a more productive second session which culminates in the endorsement of written terms of agreement.

The Written Agreement

The last stage of the mediation process is the writing of the agreement. The mediator is responsible for the organization and wording of the document. Both parties are responsible for the substance, as they are the ones who will be abiding by the terms of the agreement.

The mediator usually writes the agreement immediately after the mediation session has concluded, in the presence of both parties. The negotiations often continue during the writing process, because clarification may be needed on certain details. If the mediator perceives that it would be appropriate to write the agreement in private, he or she should ask both parties to remain nearby until the agreement has been written and typed, as the mediator may wish to check for details during the writing process.

Each party should silently read the agreement and then be afforded an opportunity to suggest changes in the final wording. The mediator must be sure that both parties understand and agree to the provisions of the document and certify that they intend to abide by it. After that has been accomplished, the document should be retyped, if necessary, photocopied, and signed by both parties and the mediator. The person signing for the school district must have the authority to carry out the provisions stipulated. If only one parent attended the mediation session, a telephone call to the other should be undertaken, if possible, for input and approval.

The agreement must be clearly written without legal or educational jargon. If either party is unsure of the wording, clarification should be requested and accomplished. Within the agreement, specifics must be addressed in terms of what services should be given, who is to give the services, when they are to be provided, and how they are to be provided. Each point should be numbered, with only one idea stated in each. Agreements should be written in a neutral tone to enhance the possibility that both parties will respect and abide by all provisions of the agreement. What follows is a hypothetical situation with two alternative examples of mediation agreements.

Mr. and Mrs. Ray Smith are dissatisfied with the progress their son, Christopher, is making in the second grade. The family has recently moved from another state where Chris was enrolled in the public school program which had an individualized education program within the regular school curriculum. He also participated in a resource gifted program for students who had individual intelligence scores of 130 or above on the Wechsler Intelligence Scale for Children–Revised.

Upon entering the River City Public Schools, Chris was placed in a section of the second grade in which instruction in all subject areas was at the second grade level. He was denied entrance into the resource program for gifted students. The parents had been told that students had to be in the school district for one year before being considered for testing and placement in programs for gifted students.

Mrs. Smith had consulted with Christopher's teacher, Mrs. Jones, and was told that her son had good second grade reading skills and that she should not worry about her son's progress. The mother related to the teacher that her son was successfully participating in all second grade academic areas in kindergarten. Each student in the previous school was annually tested to determine his or her instructional level in all academic areas and was grouped with students of like abilities. Upon completing the first grade, her son would have been in upper-level fourth grade materials. The mother further stated that it was known that many students enrolled in the River City School were gifted and perhaps the same philosophy of instruction could be adopted in her classroom. The teacher stated that changing the instructional program would be impossible and that all of the students in her class liked their materials.

Mrs. Smith then made an appointment with the principal who stated that he ran a happy school and that the parents were not complainers. He further declared that no exceptions are made to the school board policy of waiting one year to be tested for the gifted program. Mrs. Smith documented all conversations in writing.

She then made an appointment with the superintendent to see the policy on testing; he could not find a copy of it. She then called the new president of the school board who said that no such policy appeared in writing although he, as a parent, had heard the statement made several times. Further, he indicated that he too was concerned about the grade level instruction is all the schools. He did tell her that the state allowed mediation to settle disputes in education, although that provision had never been employed in the River City Schools. He gave her the name of the person serving as director of the Division of Mediation at the state level.

With diligence and perseverance, Mr. and Mrs. Smith were able to have a mediation meeting scheduled within the next ten days. It was conducted following the procedures similar to the ones just discussed, and a mediation agreement was written and signed. This particular agreement not only satisfied Mr. and Mrs. Smith, but was helpful to school personnel in implementing an educational program appropriate for Christopher. Two sample mediation agreements are presented for illustrative purposes.

Date of Mediation Session: March 18, 1990

Mediator: Mr. Henry Doe

Student's Name: Christopher Smith

Student's School: Stream Elementary School

Parents' Names: Mr. and Mrs. Ray Smith

Address: 1317 Water Road

Name of School District: River City Public Schools

Persons in attendance with the parents:

       Name, Title
       Name, Title

Persons in attendance with the school district:

       Name, Title
       Name, Title

Sample Mediation Agreement #1

In the matter of Mediation between:

Complainant: Mr. and Mrs. Ray Smith

Respondent: Mrs. Hilda Jones, second grade teacher, and Mrs. Charles White, the curriculum coordinator for elementary and secondary school programs. Both are employees of the River City School District.

AGREEMENT

We, the undersigned, having participated in a mediation session on March 19, 1990, and being satisfied that the provisions of the resolution of our dispute are fair and reasonable, hereby agree to abide by and fulfill the following:

1. Someone will test Christopher to determine his instructional level and provisions will be made for appropriate instruction.

2. A member of the staff will administer the appropriate testing for eligibility for the gifted program.

_____ Mediator/Witness

_____

_____ Parents/Guardians

_____

_____ School Official(s)

_____

_____ Date

Sample Mediation Agreement #2

In the matter of Mediation between:

Complainant: Mr. and Mrs. Ray Smith

Respondent: Mrs Hilda Jones, second grade teacher, and Mrs. Charles White, the curriculum coordinator for elementary and secondary school programs. Both are employees of the River City School District.

AGREEMENT

We, the undersigned, having participated in a mediation session on March 19, 1990, and being satisfied that the provisions of the resolution of our dispute are fair and reasonable, hereby agree to abide by and fulfill the following:

1. Mrs. Green, the education diagnostician for the River City Schools, will administer batteries of academic test to determine the instructional levels of the students. This will be completed within two weeks.

2. An individualized instructional plan will be provided for Christopher based on his instructional levels.

3. Christopher will be placed in the appropriate grades for his academic instructional levels and he will remain in the second grade for nonacademic subjects. This will be completed within three weeks.

4. Dr. Johnson, the school psychologist, will administer to Christopher the Wechsler Intelligence Scale for Children–Revised, within the next week. If Christopher scores 130 or above on the Full Scale, he will be declared eligible for the gifted program and an IEP will be written; he will immediately be placed in the resource room program for ten hours each week.

5. Mrs. White will have the responsibility for scheduling, coordinating, and monitoring the above. If for some reason, the timetable is not met, she will put in writing the reasons for the delays with a new time line. If the delay is not acceptable to Mr. and Mrs. Smith, they have all the testing completed privately at the expense of the River City School District.

Sample Mediation Agreement #2 (continued)

6. All communications with the appropriate teachers will be conducted by Mrs. White in writing. Copies must be forwarded to Mr. and Mrs. Smith. They have the right to request another mediation session if the agreements herein are not followed.

7. Christopher will be tested annually in all academic subjects within one week of the beginning of school and will be placed at his appropriate instructional levels.

8. If for some reason Mrs. White is no longer in her present position, the superintendent will appoint the then current coordinator of curriculum for the River City Schools or a person having the same administrative responsibilities to coordinate the appropriate instructional programs for Christopher Smith.

_____ Mediator/Witness

_____

_____ Parents/Guardians

_____

_____ School Official(s)

_____

_____ Date

While both of the two preceding mediation agreements were written in response to Mr. and Mrs. Smith's concerns about the education of their son, Christopher, there are several reasons why the second is preferred over the first. Although both documents indicate that a mediation meeting was conducted and an agreement was reached, the first example lacks details. The second agreement offers specific solutions and the detailed steps to be taken. The first is written in very general terms, and therefore would not be helpful either to the parents or to the school personnel. An acceptable agreement should serve the interests of the parents and their gifted children and also be helpful to school personnel in serving the needs of the gifted.

Summary

Mediation is an excellent tool for resolving conflict and reaching agreement on the placement and education of the gifted. On behalf of the child and in the hope of renewing and maintaining favorable parental/school relationships when differences arise over the education of the gifted youngster, mediation should be given every chance to resolve the conflict before resorting to more formal approaches. Even though amiable agreements are achieved in the overwhelming majority of instances in which mediation is employed, situations do arise within which the most competent mediator has little chance of bringing about agreements between the parties in dispute. After every effort has been made without success, first through direct parent/school conferences and negotiations and then by mediation, due process may be considered by parents and other advocates in states which make provisions for this approach to conflict resolution. This is the subject of the next chapter.

Chapter 6
References

Dispute Resolution in Education: The NJCA Mediation Model. (1982). Atlanta, GA: The Neighborhood Justice Center.

Ekstrand, R. E., & Edmister, P. (1984). Mediation: A process that works. *Exceptional Children*, 51, 2, 163-167.

Mediation in special education: A resource manual for mediators. (1982). Washington, DC: National Association of the State Directors of Special Education.

—7—

Due Process and the Gifted

During the past two decades, it has become essential that school administrators be knowledgeable about and skillful in the use of due process. The United States Supreme Court's 1967 *In Re Gault* decision reminded school officials and parents that the United States Constitution protects children as well as adults, and the 1969 *Tinker v. Des Moines School District* decision warned administrators that constitutional protections do not end at the schoolhouse door. Specifically addressing due process, the Court ruled in the 1975 case, *Goss v. Lopez*, that due process must be afforded a student prior to suspension from school.

Normally, due process is imposed on school districts by the due process clauses of the Fifth and Fourteenth Amendments or by state or federal statutes. Since states are the primary providers of public school education, the due process clause of the Fourteenth Amendment is usually the issue. This proscription declares that no state may deprive any person of due process; it includes two legal concepts. The first, which is used very little by contemporary courts, is entitled *substantive due process*. When judges examine a state action under the substantive due process microscope, they are ascertaining whether the state has valid grounds for its law. If the state can show that the action is within its constitutional powers and is reasonable, the court usually will not intervene. Generally speaking, courts are reluctant to second-guess state policy making officials.

Only when state actions touch upon a sensitive individual right such as freedom of speech, will the courts strictly scrutinize the state's statute, executive order, administrative regulation, etc. For example, in the *Tinker* case mentioned above, the US Supreme Court used the First Amendment freedom of speech clause and the due process clause of the Fourteenth Amendment to strike down as unconstitutional a school board policy banning students from wearing black arm bands to school. Students wearing the arm bands to school to protest America's involvement in the Vietnam War, the court reasoned, was "symbolic" speech and protected by the First Amendment.

Of most concern to students, parents, and school administrators is the second concept — *procedural due process.* Public education, so say the courts, is a property right of which one cannot be deprived without due process. Court decisions have spelled out what the due process clause of the Fourteenth Amendment requires. But before detailing these elements, another source of procedural due process must be mentioned.

Federal and state statutes may also impose procedural due process requirements on school districts. A good example for comparative purposes is the federal statute which requires due process hearings for handicapped children when the appropriateness of the handicapped child's education plan is at question.

Whether the due process claim has constitutional and/or statutory underpinnings, four essential elements constitute due process. Procedural due process must include:

1. Notice of the hearing;
2. Opportunity to present one's arguments;
3. An impartial hearing officer(s); and
4. A review procedure.

These four requirements seem quite simple. Actually, substantial thought and effort must be afforded each of them before they will pass constitutional or statutory acceptability.

For example, is a state education employee who is not affiliated with a local school district an impartial hearing officer? Using the legislative history of the Education of All Handicapped Children Act (EHCA) as a guide, several federal courts have answered this question negatively. That is, when the parents of handicapped children and local school districts could not agree as to what education program was best for the student, courts have held that *615(b)(2)* of the EHCA prohibits an employee of a state department of education from acting as an impartial hearing officer. Courts have also interpreted the act as prohibiting university professors who have been involved in state policy making for handicapped children from being appointed hearing officers (Sacken, 1987; Salend & Zirkel, 1984). And, as discussed in the following section concerning hearing officers in gifted programs, who selects the hearing officer is likewise a significant issue.

Procedural Due Process in the States

While children do not yet have specific constitutional due process protections because they are gifted, several states have instituted statutory due process procedures when schools and parents cannot agree on what is in the best interest of the gifted child. Implementing these procedures is a wise policy decision because if parents cannot resolve their differences with the school district through negotiation, and no due process procedures are in place, the next step may be to take the issue to court. In some instances, gifted and/or handicapped children are placed under the rubric of "exceptional" children and the statutory mandates of PL 94-142, regarding due process hearings, are followed. In other states, special due process procedures have been created for issues rising out of gifted and talented programs.

Sixteen states plus the District of Columbia, in responding to a recent survey, reported that state imposed due process procedures were available to gifted students. Those states having the same provisions for the gifted as applicable to the handicapped were Alabama, Alaska, Florida, Kansas, Louisiana, New Mexico, North Carolina, Pennsylvania, Tennessee, and West Virginia. South Dakota has due process provisions specific to the gifted. In Connec-

Due Process Procedures at the State Level

Afforded Same Provisions
As Handicapped (PL 94-142)

Alabama	Alaska
Florida	Kansas
Louisiana	New Mexico
North Carolina	Pennsylvania
Tennessee	West Virginia

District Transfer
   Indiana
   Iowa

Provisions Specific to the
Gifted
   South Dakota

Identification of Gifted
Only
   Connecticut

General Due Process
Procedures Applicable
to Gifted
   District of Columbia
   Montana
   Texas

ticut, due process for the gifted applied only to identification. In Indiana and Iowa there were provisions for transfer from one district to another under general state laws/regulations for all students including the gifted. Montana, Texas, and the District of Columbia also had provisions of a general nature. Several other states replied that due process hearings for the gifted were left entirely to the discretion of local school districts (Arkansas, Georgia, Nebraska and Virginia). Given the difficulty of contacting every school district in those states, this chapter focuses on states that have established procedures for hearings. While the hearings might initially be held at the local school district level, they are subject to state imposed guidelines. The lone exception in our discussion is Kansas which allows local school districts great discretion in carrying out hearings but collects the results of the hearings in the state education department. Hopefully, more states in the very near future will establish due process procedures for the gifted and provide a central repository for hearing officer opinions.

Of the seventeen jurisdictions reporting statewide procedures, twelve states had due process provisions that applied specifically to the gifted. Four states and the District of Columbia provided students an opportunity to argue complaints through the state's general due process procedures. That is, the gifted issues were processed administratively through due process procedures open to all students with all types of complaints.

Regardless of the scope of the procedures, all state procedures possessed commonalities. For example, procedures generally required written notice of the date and time of the hearing, made a written or electronic transcript of the hearing, allowed parents to choose whether they wanted the hearing to be open or closed, allowed the student involved in the controversy to attend if appropriate, allowed expert witnesses from both sides to testify, and permitted counsel to participate. Also, most states allowed the parents, the school district, or a state education agency to initiate the hearing. An interesting variation of the procedure exists in the District of Columbia, Iowa, and Tennessee; the adversely affected student could, on his or her initiation, request a hearing.

Procedurally, states differed significantly in the initial hearing level, jurisdiction, hearing officer selection and training, and appeal routes. The hearing level refers to the affiliation of the initial hearing officer. That is, if the hearing took place before a state department of education officer, the hearing was classified as a state hearing. In some states, hearings were before regional or local hearing officers selected under state laws and regulations.

Hearing Officer Selection and Jurisdiction

All of the states in the survey, except Iowa, used only one hearing officer in the due process hearings. Iowa selects three members of the state department of education staff to preside at the hearing. While there may be safety in numbers, because all states provide for multiple levels of appeal following the initial hearing, economy and efficiency generally dictate that a lone hearing officer is sufficient.

Most varied, and certainly potentially significant in relation to outcomes, is the manner in which hearing officers are selected. In many states the appointment process is complex and replete with safeguards. In other states, selection is quite simple.

Alabama provides an example of the latter. In that state the superintendent of education appoints the hearing officer, making certain that he or she is not employed by the school district nor has a personal or professional interest in the proceedings. The procedures used in Louisiana and New Mexico are more complex. The Louisiana Provision makes the parish (county) supervisor the appointing authority, but allows the parent the right of one refusal. The parish supervisor must make the appointment from a list of regional hearing officers approved by the state department of education.

The New Mexico selection process is even more involved. When the services of a hearing officer are required in New Mexico, the school district and the parents have five working days to mutually agree upon a candidate. If a mutual agreement cannot be reached, the department of education will provide a list of five names, and each side may strike one name from the list. The state superintendent then makes the appointment from the remaining names.

Florida has a unique hearing officer selection process (Florida Department of Education, 1986). The state has a separate department of state government entitled the Division of Administrative Hearings. This agency handles all due process hearings for the state. Hearing officers must be attorneys with a minimum of five years membership in the state bar. Other selection criteria include legal writing ability, past experience, and personal qualifications. Florida evidently places greater emphasis on legal expertise than other states, as it requires the hearing officer to be an attorney. As discussed later in this chapter, a separate state hearing officer agency is an effective way to ensure the independence and impartiality of the officer.

Hearing Officer Training and Background

Just as important as an impartial selection procedure is the proper training of hearing officers. Ideally, he or she would have knowledge of gifted education principles and some legal background regarding the conduct of a hearing. In most states the hearing officer is not a lawyer, and there seems to be no overwhelming need to require this. The educational background, however, is most important and most hearing officers come from education-related occupations.

Impartiality is a concern. All states stipulate that the hearing officer must be unbiased and not have any direct or indirect interest in the dispute. As noted above concerning hearings involving the handicapped, a question arises as to whether a state department of education staff member or a university special education faculty member should be allowed to function as a hearing officer. Because of the possible relationships between the district and the state department of education or faculty member, the safest procedure would be to exclude these persons as hearing officers. University faculty members are often called upon to assist school districts in myriad ways as consultants, in-service trainers, etc. Therefore, professional and financial ties often exist. While the federal court cases previously mentioned would not directly apply since they were construing a federal statute relating to the handicapped, the court's decisions are in the spirit of due process. Simply stated, the federal courts concluded that because of conflict of interest state education officials or university professors involved in developing special education programs and policies should not function as hearing officers.

West Virginia has an exceptional selection and training procedure for hearing officers (West Virginia Department of Education, 1985). When parents and school districts are unable to resolve their differences concerning gifted education policies, the local education agency contacts the state education department which provides the disputing parties with the names of three qualified hearing officers. Each party then strikes one name with the initiating party rejecting first. The remaining nominee acts as the hearing officer.

Persons named by the state department of education as prospective hearing officers must have a college degree, West Virginia special education certification, and professional special education experience within the past two years. Persons cannot be a hearing officer if they have any personal or professional interest in the proceeding. Each hearing officer must complete a training program in the proper conduct of hearings. West Virginia (1985) has prepared an excellent and detailed manual. Written for hearing officers presiding over Public Law 94-142 cases, the manual has applicability to all due process hearings involving exceptional children, which in West Virginia encompasses gifted students.

Appeals Process

Our survey revealed that appeals from the due process hearing follow various paths. In Alabama, Iowa, South Dakota, Tennessee, and West Virginia, appeals went directly into the state court system. Seven states, however, route the appeals through the Department of Education or Superintendent of Education, and two states handle due process appeals through a special agency. Louisiana has a Special Education Review Panel, where New Mexico has a state administrative review officer. If the dispute cannot be finalized at these agencies, a party then may take the appeal to the appropriate state court.

Because there is no federal statute mandating gifted education, appeals from gifted due process hearings most often enter the state, not the federal, court system. However, if the child were gifted and also handicapped, there would be federal jurisdiction under PL 94-142. Other considerations may also open the federal courts to the gifted. For example, issues involving racial discrimination in gifted programs have been tried in the federal courts.

Subject Matter Jurisdiction of State Hearing Officers

Alabama, Alaska, Florida, Kansas, Louisiana, New Mexico, North Carolina, Pennsylvania, Tennessee, and West Virginia have established due process procedures for the gifted that approximate those of the handicapped and are under the guidelines for exceptional children.

Connecticut applies the due process procedures set forth for the handicapped to the gifted, but limits the jurisdiction only to identification. This limited subject matter jurisdiction was the issue in a 1988 Connecticut hearing; the hearing officer interpreted the Connecticut law on allowing hearing officers only to render decisions concerning the identification of the gifted. The determination was that Connecticut law did limit hearings to identification.

South Dakota has a provision specific to academic giftedness which provides for a three-member mediation team; this team determines if the child qualifies for special services, either through an adjustment in the regular curriculum or whether the student qualifies for additional services involving an individual educational plan. While South Dakota labels the initial step a mediation process in a dispute involving a gifted child, this team functions more like a due process hearing panel than as mediators (Chapter Six discussed the differences between a mediation and a due process hearing). Appeals from the mediation team are reviewed by the state superintendent of education.

In the state of Indiana, gifted students do not come under the definition of exceptional children, but there is a general provision for hearings to be conducted for any student needing a transfer from one school district to another. To date, three hearings have been held in Indiana involving the transfer of gifted and talented students. These are described in the following section on hearing officer decisions.

In Iowa, there is a statute which provides for appropriate instructional program review. Hearings may be held when the student has been or is about to be denied entry or continuance into an instructional program appropriate to his or her needs. Hearings are also possible if the student has been or is about to be required to enter or continue in a program which is inappropriate to his or her individual needs. As discussed later in this chapter, parents have used this general provision to request hearings for their gifted children.

The District of Columbia Public Schools do not provide specific due process procedures for the gifted. However, under provisions in the rules of the board of education, hearings may be conducted for any student under a general grievance procedure (1) when a student or a group of students is denied an adequate educational opportunity; (2) when the right of a student(s) is being subjected to an arbitrary or unreasonable regulation; and (3) when a student(s) is being denied the opportunity to participate in any school activity for which he or she is eligible. No hearings to date have involved gifted students.

Texas administrative regulations contain a general provision for the hearing of appeals brought on any matter of dispute based on the school laws of the state or on any actions or decisions of any board of trustees or board of education. The appeal for a hearing is made to the Commissioner of Education. A hearing using this statute in a gifted education dispute is discussed in the next section. Thus far there has been only one hearing conducted on behalf of a gifted student.

In Arkansas, Georgia, Nebraska, and Virginia, due process hearings are limited to the discretion of the local school districts. The remaining states indicate that there are no specific provisions for due process for the gifted, either at the local or state levels. Because opportunities for due process are so valuable, gifted education advocates should consult the last part of this chapter for ideas on implementing a due process system.

Hearing Officer Decisions

Tracking down specific hearing officer decisions on gifted students was not easy. We found the decisions in a variety of places, including the offices of the chief education officers, state consultants for the gifted, and the attorneys general. In at least one situation, the parents provided us with the decision. In some instances the written decision of the hearing officer was provided while some states only reported interpretations of the decisions by state officials. Most states retained confidentiality of due process discussions by deleting the names of the children, parents and the hearing officers. In many situations the designation of the school district was also withheld. Therefore, the following descriptions of due process hearings are general in nature.

Alabama

Four due process hearings for gifted students were reported for Alabama. Three hearings involved eligibility for admission into a gifted program. Two of these eligibility hearings were decided in favor of the parents, with the gifted child granted admission to specialized programs. In the other eligibility case, the child was denied admission based on the variance in intelligence test scores. The fourth hearing illustrates that parents sometimes emerge with a favorable response even when the original relief sought was denied. In this dispute, parents who sought private school placement for their gifted child due to a lack of direct services in the public school were denied relief. However, the public school district was required by the hearing officer to hire a certified teacher or consultant for the gifted.

Alaska

In Alaska one hearing has been reported. The mother was denied her request to have her gifted child taught a curriculum that the parent deemed appropriate.

Indiana

As mentioned, due process in Indiana is limited to the transfer of a student to a district with an appropriate program. This provision is afforded to all students. Of the three hearings in the school year 1986–1987, only one student was granted the transfer. The hearing officer granted the transfer based on the finding that the student would be better "accommodated" by the curriculum offerings at the new school. One was denied the transfer because the current school district provided curriculum offerings substantially similar to the requested school. The other was denied for the same reason; in addition, there was not space available at the requested school. A 1988 hearing officer decision permitted a tenth grade gifted student to transfer to another school district to take advantage of an established gifted program and a more intellectually challenging curriculum.

Iowa

As previously described, Iowa allows for hearings for all students based on the concept of appropriateness of instruction. Six hearings have been conducted with five decisions favoring the parents. In two cases, tuition was granted for the student to attend another school district; in three cases the districts were directed to pay tuition for placement in another district or provide appropriate instruction. In the last hearing, the child enrolled in a gifted program was prohibited from transferring to another district's program for the gifted.

Kansas

Hearing officer decisions in Kansas are made at the district level by a person appointed by the local school board rather than at the state level. Hearing officers selected by the local school board have been staff members of the Legal Aid Society or faculty members at a state university. All hearings conducted thus far have involved placement in a gifted program. Five decisions have denied eligibility and two were delayed until more testing could be completed.

A January 1989 hearing is representative of the Kansas hearings. In this controversy, parents contested the district's decision not to admit the child to a gifted program. At the hearing stage of the dispute, a hearing officer, relying on testimony presented by the child's teacher and other expert witnesses, ruled that the child met the established Kansas standards to be identified as a gifted student and ordered the child admitted to the gifted program. In a well-written decision, the hearing officer placed substantial weight on the third-grade teacher's evaluation that the child displayed a great deal of originality, creativity, and curiosity in her classroom work.

Louisiana

Reported for Louisiana were seven due process hearings with six appeals. Four hearings dealt with the issue of placement or continuing placement with two decisions favoring the parents. The third hearing on placement was dismissed because it was deemed premature. In the fourth, a federal court desegregation order negated a hearing officer's decision that a child be placed in a gifted program at a magnet school, because it could perpetuate a racial imbalance. In a fifth hearing, after a hearing officer determined that a student was not receiving appropriate services and ordered a teacher hired, the review panel stated that the school board had the right to determine the setting for the delivery of services. Therefore, the school board had the option of selecting the method of delivery of appropriate services, i.e., placement in another school, transfer to a magnet school, or the hiring of an additional teacher. The review panel, however, informed the parents to notify the state department of education immediately if appropriate services were not provided.

In the sixth hearing and second involving the issue of appropriate education, a hearing officer ruled that any reduction of academic content was not an appropriate program. In this case the school system had reduced an academic instructional program by fifty-five minutes for all students. This ruling was reversed by the review panel in appeal. The panel concluded that the hearing officer ruling placed the burden of proof about the appropriateness of any program on the school board. Rather than a question of a burden of proof, the special education appeals panel stated that the real issue in a due process hearing was the appropriate education of the specific child.

In an early admission hearing, a Louisiana hearing officer ordered that a hearing impaired gifted child be placed in kindergarten for the second semester. The review panel held that there were no provisions for a January entrance into kindergarten and the child should be retained in the early childhood education program.

North Carolina

North Carolina reported six due process hearings from 1970 through 1988. The parents in one instance challenged the appropriateness of an individual educational plan and it was ruled appropriate. In two hearings it was determined that a child previously ruled eligible for a gifted program was properly excluded, because of reevaluation data reported in the hearing. In two other hearings, decisions were delayed because more testing information was requested. In a final case, although the parents requested placing the student in both the science and mathematics program, the hearing officer decided to place him only in a science program for the gifted.

Pennsylvania

Pennsylvania has had the largest number of due process hearings. Information provided by the Right to Education Office in that state indicated that within a fifteen year span, there were sixty-nine due process hearings. Twenty-seven, or approximately 40 percent, of the hearing officers' decisions were appealed. The data revealed that hearing officers' decisions on behalf of the gifted were appealed more frequently than hearings involving the handicapped. These decisions dealt with eligibility, appropriateness of the individual educational plan, and the appropriateness of instruction.

Two disputes deserve special mention. One reveals how the perseverance of parents, when informed that the school district was financially unable to provide services for their children, eventually resulted in the delivery of services. The second dispute indicates how the tenacity of the parent of one child benefitted other gifted students in that district.

The first dispute involved eight families whose children were identified as gifted but were denied participation in the district's pullout program. Because the pullout program was full and the district had been denied additional state funding for their gifted program, the district provided two options, neither of which satisfied the parents of the eight children.

The first option was to have the children receive a gifted enrichment program within the regular classroom, and the second alternative was to have the children participate in the itinerant pullout program beginning the next academic year (1989–1990). Dissatisfied with the choices, the parents requested a due process hearing. At the conclusion of the May 3, 1989 hearing, the school district agreed to employ the gifted education teacher for an additional quarter time at the district's expense. Employing the teacher for this additional time provided room for the eight students to participate in the pullout program for the balance of the 1988–1989 school year. The outcome in this case is significant because districts often use budgetary considerations as a reason for denying services. In this case, the parents persevered and were able to overcome the budgetary obstacle.

The second hearing had collateral consequences which required the school district to improve its gifted education services. At issue in this dispute was a high school senior's request to leave school early to participate in a community theater program. Identified as gifted in the third grade, the student had not had an Individualized Education Plan (IEP) since the seventh grade. When the student was denied the request to leave school early, the parents requested an IEP.

A prehearing conference was held in November, 1988, but the parent and the district could not agree on a valid IEP. After continued negotiations and extraordinary delay, a hearing was scheduled for August, 1989. Unfortunately for the student, by the time the hearing was held, she had graduated from high school leaving the release time issue moot. The hearing officer did state that the student would have had a stronger case if she had obtained a part in a theater production; more importantly, the hearing officer admonished the district for their lapse in time in providing an IEP for the student. Such a lapse, the hearing officer concluded, denied the student a free and appropriate program of special education. As a portion of the final order, the hearing officer instructed the district to disseminate, within thirty days, an informational brochure describing the rights of the gifted children under due process to all parents of the district's gifted children. In this instance, one parent's attempt to win a specific right for her child conceivably benefitted an entire group of gifted children.

South Dakota

During 1988 and 1989 in South Dakota, there were five hearings regarding gifted education. Interestingly, four of the five hearings involved children in one family. The hearings involved a change of state definition, and the district contended that the students were no longer eligible based on the new definition. The hearing officer ruled that the children were gifted and referred the issue to the placement committee. The other hearing involved a student with outstanding abilities in mathematics, and the decision was to pro-

vide instruction through a properly formulated individualized educational plan.

Tennessee

In Tennessee, due process hearings span three decades. Zettel
(1979) discusses a 1975 Tennessee hearing involving the question
of a "free and appropriate public education" for a gifted child. In
this hearing the parents won the right to be present at a conference
to determine the appropriate education for their son. In a 1982 case,
a high school student, declared as gifted in 1979, was held not to
be gifted based on current intelligence test scores. The hearing
officer upheld the decision of the local school district. In another
hearing the parents of a fourth grade gifted child sought placement
of their child at the fifth grade level. The hearing officer determined
the current grade placement was appropriate, but that counseling
should be added to the individualized educational plan. In another
dispute, parents sought placement of their gifted child in an accelerated second grade class. The hearing officer determined an appropriate individualized educational plan needed to be written and the
parents must be reimbursed for attorney's fees. In an early admission
controversy, after the parents had obtained a hearing officer mandate
for their four-year-old child to be given school district services, the
LEA appealed the decision to a chancery court in Tennessee. When
the judge ordered another due process hearing, the parents chose
not to pursue it.

In a significant 1986 due process hearing in Tennessee, the hearing
officer ruled that the gifted child should have an IEP developed for
her which would go beyond the minimum pullout enrichment program. This decision further stated that the goals of the IEP must
have measurable objectives in all areas based upon assessment with
specified instruments. The hearing officer also ruled that the school
system reimburse the parents' expenses in hiring a consultant/advo-
cate. The tuition costs for time spent in a private school were denied.
The school district appealed the hearing officer's decision on the
reimbursement for the consultant advocate to a Tennessee Chancery
Court. The judge denied the reimbursement of these expenses

based on the fact that the advocate was not an attorney.

In a 1990 due process hearing in the same state, the hearing officer ruled that a sixth grade student, who had been denied placement in a gifted program, was not properly screened to be certified as gifted. Two out of three criteria had to be met in order to be ruled eligible for the special services. The student qualified on the criteria of the objective achievement testing, but did not on the objective intelligence testing. The third criteria involved the subjective evaluation of the student's intellectual abilities. There had not been a classroom observation of the child's performance by a member of the evaluation team. Therefore, the hearing officer ruled that the student was entitled to a reevaluation under proper procedures.

Texas

In Texas, the parents of a middle school gifted student sought continuation of placement in a high school program for the gifted. The criteria for placement at each level in the programs were different and the child missed the required minimum on the Stanford Achievement Test (SAT) by just a few points. The Commissioner of Education as the hearing officer determined that the items for identifying students for the secondary program were legally and professionally acceptable. The parents refused to have their child retake the SAT, and therefore the student was denied access to the English program for gifted students at the secondary level.

West Virginia

Since 1985, according to the West Virginia Department of Education, three due process hearings have been reported with two appeals. One hearing involved a gifted kindergarten student whose parents requested that he be placed in the first grade. The hearing officer's decision was that the kindergarten placement was appropriate; the parents requested an administrative appeal. By the time this occurred, the child had completed his kindergarten year. The reviewing officer recommended grade level acceleration for the second semester of the first grade experience. This decision was further reviewed by the West Virginia Board of Education who upheld the judgment of the reviewing official.

The remaining West Virginia hearings concerned two older students and the implementation of the individual educational plans. The parents of a middle school gifted female student stated that the IEP was not being implemented as written. The hearing officer ruled that the IEP was appropriate, but that a complete reevaluation be conducted by an independent qualified examiner. Upon review, it was determined that specificity be given to a new IEP and that a facilitator of gifted education be appointed to oversee the implementation. The hearing officer report further stated that both the cognitive and affective needs of the student be addressed. Services should be provided to help the student in dealing positively with her giftedness and the pressures generated by her unique program.

In the second hearing, the IEP of a gifted seventeen-year-old high school senior was found to be appropriate by an impartial hearing officer and by the reviewing official. However, the latter ordered that a resource teacher for the gifted be added to the IEP in order to implement the program as written.

Gifted and Handicapped

Two additional due process hearings from Maryland and Massachusetts need to be mentioned. Although these hearings were held in states which reported that they do not provide due process specifically for the gifted, the hearings involved gifted/handicapped students and the hearing officers' decisions are victories for gifted education proponents.

The Maryland hearing was held under the guidelines of PL 94-142 and Section 504 of the Rehabilitation Act of 1973, as amended, 29 U.S.C. 794. A Baltimore Public School district child had been identified as both gifted and learning disabled. Because the child did not make progress in the first grade in reading, language, and mathematics, the district recommended removal of the child from the Gifted and Talented Education (GATE) program. At the parent-initiated due process hearing, the local hearing officer ruled the child should be excluded from the GATE program. Dissatisfied with this decision, the parents requested a hearing at the state level. The Maryland State Department of Education hearing officer reversed the local hearing officer decision and ordered the child to remain in the GATE program. Section 504 of the Rehabilitation Act, the hearing officer concluded, prohibited the child's exclusion from the gifted curriculum because of her handicapping condition. Instead, the school district must provide special reading services for the child as well as allow her to participate in the gifted program. Because many states restrict the variety of services provided the gifted/handicapped student, this hearing officer decision indicates an enlightened approach in exceptional child education.

The Massachusetts hearing was also conducted under the provisions of PL 94-142 and the state law for special education. The parents of a kindergarten student with a high intelligence test score contended that the discrepancies between the Verbal and Performance scores on the Wechsler Intelligence Scale for Children–Revised (WISC-R) rendered him a student with special needs and entitled him to special education services. After the district claimed that the student could progress academically and socially within the regular classroom, the parents requested a due process hearing.

The hearing officer ruled that the evidence did not support the finding that the student needed special education services for a learning disability, but sufficient questions were raised regarding the student's weaknesses in the visual-motor skills to necessitate limited special education intervention. Because the child had a Full Scale intelligence quotient on the WISC-R of 141, the hearing officer requested that the student's progress within the regular classroom be monitored to ensure enrichment services and/or an individualized curriculum.

Analysis of Due Process Procedures and Decisions Involving Gifted Youth

Ten states use the same due process procedures for the gifted as they do for the handicapped. Another state applies the procedures used for the handicapped but limits the question to identification.

One state has procedures designed specifically for the gifted and four states and the District of Columbia have settled disputes involving gifted students under procedures generally applicable to all students. From information supplied by state officials and others, there have been approximately one-hundred due process hearings conducted over the last fifteen years on behalf of gifted youth, with approximately half of them being held in the state of Pennsylvania. Hearings have generally been conducted for purposes of identification; appropriateness of placement; appropriateness of programming, including individual educational plans; and the transfer of students to districts having appropriate services. As states or the federal government mandate gifted education, certainly more due process hearings will be conducted.

Based upon our research, there were commonalties among the due process hearings according to the data in the survey. In all states, the opportunity to begin the procedures was given to both the parent and the school. In a few states, it was allowable for the student to initiate the request for a hearing. State regulations provided that sufficient notice, usually written, be provided the participants. All states allowed for electronic and/or written transcripts of the hearings. In some cases, the parent had to request a transcript of the hearing. Another common feature of the due process procedures was that specific time lines for conducting the hearings and the issuance of decisions were stated. All states provided ample opportunity for both parties, parents and school authority, to present relevant evidence and witnesses.

Our examination of due process procedures established in each state suggests that some areas need improvement. Appropriate decision makers such as state legislators, state boards of education, and courts should review the following due process procedures. Which decision maker will have the responsibility for review will depend on the statutes, rules and regulations, and court precedents in that state. Because of the difficulty in securing information on due process hearings, communication on the process and/or outcomes of the hearing should be disseminated to all persons at the state and local levels who need the information to effectively perform their duties. It is in the best interest of educators and parents to share their information. While all the states allow the parents to make the decision as to whether the hearing should be open or closed, the subject matter and the decision should be disseminated without the names of the parties. This would allow educators, parents, and other interested parties to have information concerning the activities in this area and establish a body of knowledge. State Department of Education officials should make certain that procedures are in place to distribute these decisions.

A major communication problem is that the written opinions of the hearing officer decisions often lack clarity in style and content. In some instances, these opinions are only one paragraph long and announce only the decisions. This brevity provides little guidance to educators, parents, and appellate agencies as to the issues involved, and the rationale for the decisions. Another area of concern is the laxity in scoring tests. In several situations incorrect scoring resulted in hearings being conducted needlessly.

A greater concern has to do with the staffing of the hearing officer position. Since there is often an ongoing relationship between the school district and the state department of education, it would promote impartiality if someone other than a state department of education official functioned as a hearing officer. A similar concern involves university faculty members serving as hearing officers, because in some cases faculty members serve as consultants to local and state educational agencies in developing programs for the gifted and, therefore, have a vested interest. Also, to avoid the taint of partiality, paid local or regional officials should not have the responsibility of appointing hearing officers because of a possible conflict of interest.

To date, most states conducting due process hearings involving the gifted do not require the hearing officer to be an attorney. A hearing need not, and should not, be as technical as a trial. Most lawyers do not have knowledge of the laws and policies governing gifted education; therefore, to have an effective due process procedure, hearing officer training is an integral part of the system. Training in the legal principles and the knowledge of educational issues must be sufficient to conduct a fair and impartial hearing. Essential to good training programs is the requirement that hearing officers receive continuing education on a regular basis. West Virginia is an example of a state having such a requirement.

Most states provide that appeals of the decisions of the hearing officers be entrusted to a person or department in the state educational agency. To avoid the apparent conflict of interest, a better procedure would be to establish a panel of three hearing officers outside the department of education to review a hearing officer decision. These review boards could be established by creating a division of administrative hearings.

The review boards could be located in a state agency which had broad subject matter jurisdiction and whose mission is to process hearings from all state agencies. Or, if such a separate structure were not feasible, the review board could be a specifically designated panel of gifted education hearing officers. If the latter appeal procedure is used, the hearing officers should be selected on a rotating basis from a state department of education list and reside outside the jurisdiction where the controversy arose. Appeals after the review board decision would be to the state or federal courts.

Of the two models of review board appeal described, the first provides the greatest appearance of fairness. A state agency which is completely independent of the state education department removes any inherent taint of injustice. While there is a concern that a hearing officer or a review panel would not possess expertise in gifted education, sufficient understanding of the subject to conduct a hearing or review of a hearing could be readily obtained.

Why not direct a review of the due process hearing by the courts rather than a review board which creates another tier in the bureaucracy? The answer is simply that attorneys and courts result in added expense and delay. Given the overburdened judicial system, the courts should truly be a last resort after all other remedies have failed.

Recommendations for Implementing Due Process

The states providing due process for the gifted have initiated a positive means for both the school districts and the parents in the settlement of disputes. For those states needing to update and/or expand their procedures, and for states wanting to develop a due process model, we offer the following recommendations

The first step is to review any state and federal statutes with accompanying rules and regulations, and relevant court cases. This will determine whether or not the existing model is in compliance with current state law. If there is a disparity, this research will provide a legal foundation for requesting school officials to adhere to existing law.

Essential to any model are the following components: jurisdiction; selection, background, and training of the hearing officer; procedures for conducting the hearing and issuing the decisions; and the steps in the appeal process. The jurisdiction component should include provisions for screening/identification of the gifted, programming in both the regular school enterprise and the special education provisions outside the regular classroom, the individual educational plan, evaluation, and other specifications as deemed appropriate. Another key component that some states lack is a system for collecting and reporting the hearing officer decisions. As part of the model, a uniform, statewide format should be developed for the writing of such decisions. All decisions should be transmitted to a central office within the state department of education.

A committee consisting of such persons as the state consultant(s) in gifted education, teachers and school administrators from the public school sector, university and college faculty, representatives of the state association(s) for the gifted and talented, an educational liaison officer from the office of the attorney general, a lawyer for the state board of education, and other appropriate representatives of gifted children should be appointed to develop the model.

After the model has been developed by the appropriate state decision makers, the implementation phase begins. There needs to be a plan to train the hearing officers. This should include the criteria for selection of those to be trained and the development of a handbook for the training with possible simulation materials, such as videotapes. Provisions should also be stated for the continuing education of the hearing officers. Colleges and universities could provide technical assistance to the state departments of education for the initial and continuing training of the hearing officers and school district personnel.

The general awareness campaign for implementing the model should be in two phases. All professional school district staff should be provided with detailed written information on due process. This information should be distributed at meetings where all roles are delineated and opportunity for discussion provided. Parents should be informed through printed material describing their opportunities to initiate the due process mechanism. A series of seminars should be conducted for parents for the purpose of disseminating the information. Awareness activities for both the public schools and the parents should be conducted on an annual basis. A plan for all activities should be developed and evaluated by the statewide committee.

Finally, it is essential that the due process model be closely monitored. Parents, teachers, public school officials, college and university faculty, and other concerned citizens should be vigilant to make certain the system is operating properly. This will ensure that the same procedures are in place statewide and provide state education department officials suggestions for improving the model. Such monitoring should include the search for any changes in applicable state law brought about by legislative, administrative, or court modification.

For informational purposes, hearing officer decisions should be made available upon request to interested parties. This will allow parents, hearing officers, school district personnel, and others to understand the content and procedure involved in hearing officer decisions. If the number of hearings warrant it, a state department of education report providing the types and number of hearing officer decisions should be issued annually.

Recommended Due Process Models

We have included two due process models which could be used to resolve gifted education disputes. As noted above, it will vary among the states who will have the responsibility for creating these models. In some states it can be done by specific legislative action, or in other states, it could be accomplished by state boards of education acting under general legislative guidelines. Litigations could result in a judge interpreting a general education statute, imposing due process for the gifted upon a state. It would be much better, of course, if the representatives of the people serving in the legislature initiated the due process system, which would be quicker and have general application throughout the state compared to court action involving specific parties. Note that both models offer ample opportunities to settle disputes during the initial stages of the controversy. This level is where, if at all possible, the controversy should end.

A key to successful resolution is the opportunity to have meaningful parent-teacher conferences. If these talks fail, then there should be an opportunity for program supervisors and building administrators to enter the discussion. If no agreement can be reached at this stage, the school district should offer a mediation procedure. As noted in Chapter Six, this procedure needs to be structured so that the mediators involved are impartial and professionally trained. Only after these two stages fail should the more formal and expensive due process hearing be pursued.

The key element to the entire due process hearing is the hearing officer. This person must be sufficiently trained in legal matters and gifted education so that both procedural fairness and knowledgeable decisions can be obtained. Model A suggests that a hearing officer be selected from a state government agency responsible for providing hearing officers for all types of due process hearings. These persons would be attorneys trained sufficiently in various subject matters so that they possessed substantive knowledge concerning several technical areas of law including education. This model follows what has occurred recently at the federal administrative law judge level. Rather than serving as hearing officers for only

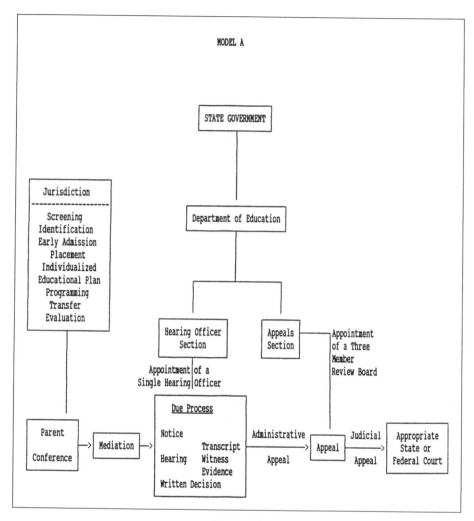

Figure 4

one agency, federal administrative law judges now hold hearings in several different fields. At the state level, Florida now utilizes such a system.

In addition to independence and fairness, Model A has several other advantages. The hearing officers are not tied to one agency so they can be efficiently and effectively allocated throughout the state governmental system; they would possess both technical and substantive expertise; and when appeals were filed, they would present a pool from which review panel officers could be chosen. The review board panel could be located in the same agency but consist of a separate section within that agency.

Model B presents a slight variation pertaining to the source for

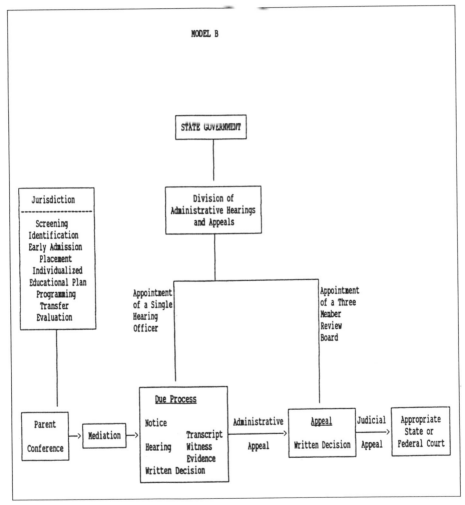

Figure 5

hearing officers. If states do not have a centralized hearing officer division, then they should be selected from a list maintained by the state education department. Hearing officers on this list should receive training in legal and gifted education concepts. Review board members should be selected from separate hearing officer lists on a rotating basis.

Models A and B provide the opportunity for aggrieved parties to settle a dispute without resorting to the courts. Both models provide an infrastructure to settle disputes successfully that cannot be easily resolved. If the dispute cannot be settled at the due process level, or the state does not provide such a procedure, then the dissatisfied party may take the dispute to the courts. A procedurally sound and operating due process system can save parents and school systems thousands of dollars, a great amount of time and, most important, speed the delivery of appropriate educational services to the gifted child.

Chapter 7
References

Education of All Handicapped Children Act, 20 U.S.C. 1415(b)(2) (1982).

Estrand, R. E., P. Edmister, & J. Riggin. (1989). *Preparation for special education hearings: A practical guide to lessening the trauma of due process hearings.* Reston, VA: The Council for Exceptional Children.

Goss v. Lopez, 419 U.S. (1975).

Hearing officers due process manual. (1985). Charleston, WV: West Virginia Department of Education.

In Re Gault, 387 U.S. 1 (1967).

Rehabilitation Act of 1973, S 504, 29 U.S.C. S 794 (1982).

Resource manual for the development and evaluation of special programs for exceptional students, Vol. III-C: Mediation and due process procedures (1986). Tallahassee, FL: Department of Education.

Sacken, D. (1987). *Mayson v. Teague*: The dilemma of selecting hearing officers. *Journal of Law and Education, 16*(2), 187-201.

Salend, S., & P. Zirkel. (1984). Special education hearings: Prevailing problems and practical proposals. *Education and Training of the Mentally Retarded, 19*(1), 29-34.

Tinker v. Des Moines, 393 U.S. 503 (1969).

Zettel, J. (1979). State provisions for educating the gifted and talented. In A. W. Passow (Ed.), *The Gifted and The Talented* (pp. 63-74). Chicago: University of Chicago Press.

—8—

Current and Future Legal Issues
in Gifted Education

The legal process will undoubtedly be used in the future to bring greater protection for gifted children and youth. The states will continue to enact new statutes, court decisions, rules and regulations affecting gifted children. But even with the new statutes and their interpretation, gifted education advocates will find it essential that they pursue appropriate mediation, due process, and litigation if the gifted and talented are to have ample opportunity for appropriate quality education.

Several issues surround the chronological ages of gifted children and youth and an appropriate education. In the states which have no exceptions to the early admissions statutes, and/or policies and procedures, parents may have to resort to the legal process to allow students early access to the public schools. These ensuing disputes may focus on two problems. The first is one of early admission to preschool and kindergarten programs. Although there are states which have standards for early admission, some allow the local districts to determine if they wish to adopt policies and procedures which permit exceptions to the admission age specified. In a few states, there may be no alternatives except a court order. The second type of early admission dispute involves the gifted students' attendance at a postsecondary institution. The availability or nonavailability of early admission avenues may lead to several types of conflicts.

Possible disputes involving early admission to postsecondary institutions would include, but not be limited to:

1. Whether state law may limit the age at which an elementary or secondary gifted or talented student may be enrolled in a postsecondary institution;

2. Whether an elementary or secondary school age student enrolled in a postsecondary program may use the credits earned in college toward a high school diploma;

3. Whether such a student graduating from a secondary school can receive an honors and/or a valedictorian designation;

4. Whether a student in an elementary or secondary school whose educational needs are beyond the curriculum offered may attend a postsecondary institution when state law requires secondary school attendance until reaching a specified age;

5. Whether a designated number of Carnegie Units can be required before a student may be considered for early admission to a postsecondary institution when other standards have been met; and

6. Whether state law requiring mandatory school attendance prohibits enrollment in a postsecondary institution.

Many problems will continue to arise in connection with the screening and identification of gifted and talented students. These controversies will require attention, definition, and clarification. With the passage of the new federal law on gifted education, Jacob K. Javits Gifted and Talented Students Education Act of 1988, and its emphasis on serving youth in lower socioeconomic circumstances, and the gifted in rural areas and minorities, it is now essential that efforts be redoubled to search out, screen, identify, admit, and serve effectively the eligible, to be found in substantial number, in groups heretofore seriously neglected. Implementation of the provisions of this new law will not necessarily give rise to a whole new set of issues and problems, but will most assuredly focus attention on some of the most critical and difficult of the complex problems confronting the gifted and the total educational enterprise.

Eligibility Criteria

Gifted and talented students come from various social, economic, racial, ethnic backgrounds, and with handicapping conditions.

Questions will continue to arise as to whether nondiscriminatory testing procedures have been used for those students who do not have English as their first language and for those who may not perform well on traditional measures because of cultural diversity or handicap.

In those states in which students, outstanding in the areas of fine and performing arts, must or may be served under provisions of gifted education, the question emerges as to who conducts the screening and identification. This is a sensitive issue. In some states, professionals in the specific area of the arts have the responsibility for the identification of those students to be considered eligible for services. When they are not designated, who has the professional competencies to determine those students eligible for special services?

Using a single criterion for identification may be subject to a legal challenge. Therefore, caution should be stressed when eligibility is determined by a single test score. Past court decisions suggest that multiple criteria should be employed.

Problems frequently arise when states and local districts establish one set of criteria for admission to, or retention in, one type of program for the gifted and different criteria for another. Because states and districts have the option of adopting criteria which vary from one program to another or changing admission and continuation requirements, conflicts may arise when parents and others are not informed of changes in advance. An example of this would be a change in eligibility criteria for admission to programs from the elementary to secondary levels.

Another sensitive problem for possible legal consideration is the disparity of eligibility criteria from district to district within a state and from one state to another. The latter may be more readily defended because of the autonomy of each state in the development of definition and criteria. The differences in criteria from district to district within a given state may be more open to legal scrutiny.

Concerns about how tests are administered have sometimes proven legitimate. Every effort should be made to properly score all measures used in the screening and identification process. On occasion, psychologists and other school personnel do make computational mistakes. No child should be denied services based on improper scoring of tests and/or mathematical error. This issue has been the focus of gifted education disputes.

Teacher Certification

Both school personnel and parents will be interested in the legal developments regarding the certification/endorsement of gifted teachers. There currently appear to be three approaches. Approximately one-half of the states do not have certification/endorsement standards in gifted education, thus require no specialized training beyond basic certification to conduct special classes for the gifted. In a few states, there is certification/endorsement, but it is optional. In the remaining states, specific certification/endorsement requirements in gifted education have been developed and implemented. Gifted education is only one of a few areas of education where teachers in every state are not required to have specialized course work and training in their area of instructional responsibility.

In states where certification/endorsement in gifted education is not mandatory, two legal issues are emerging. The first concerns a teacher trained in gifted education being replaced in the gifted program when the district faces financial difficulties. The program may be continued but staffed with a teacher who lacks appropriate credentials. Understandably, the trained teacher may feel a complaint is warranted. The second legal issue focuses on the same problem, but from a different perspective. When parents witness a qualified teacher being replaced by one lacking a background in gifted education they become concerned about the quality and continuity of the program and may seek legal recourse.

An additional question about certification/endorsement involves gifted education training for the regular classroom teacher. If states are requiring teachers in specialized programs to have additional knowledge and methodologies for the gifted students they are responsible for during a short period of time each week, should not there be additional knowledge and methodological training required of the regular classroom teacher, who is responsible for their instruction the majority of the school year? With such training, teachers would possess the subject matter depth and could also effectively coordinate the material to be taught with the rate and style of learning of gifted students. Thus, the certification/endorsement of all teachers serving the gifted may be an issue in the future.

Delivery of Services

In states that require an individualized education plan (IEP), conflicts may arise. Questions will emerge as to the appropriateness of the delivery of services based on the needs of the student as to whether they should be provided through enrichment in the regular classroom, part-time special class, full-time special class, independent study, itinerant teacher, mentorships, resource rooms, special schools, early entrance, continuous progress, nongraded school, moderate acceleration, radical acceleration, College Board Advanced Placement, fast paced courses, or concurrent or dual enrollment. A definition of related services as required to be included in some IEPs may also have to be determined.

If a child is identified as having needs beyond the offerings of the school district, must the district expand its curriculum to meet those needs? The Pennsylvania courts have said no, but this is an issue that will be raised repeatedly in the future. If the district cannot meet the curricular needs of the student, and if the school is not required to expand the course offerings, should the youth have a right to transfer to another school district? The transfer from one school district to another based on the need for advanced instruction will be a persistent question in gifted education.

If a school transfer is not feasible, another option at the secondary level involves the student being dually enrolled, or admitted as a full time student, at a postsecondary institution at the cost of the school district when an appropriate education cannot be provided for the gifted youth. Currently in Louisiana this option may be written into the IEP with the financial responsibility borne by the public schools. Parents in other states will possibly be seeking a similar option.

Also in regard to curriculum, many of these students spend the majority of time in school in the regular classroom. Although they are capable of learning concepts beyond those taught at their grade level, few are offered the opportunity for learning at their instructional level with some form of acceleration. As gifted education proponents become more sensitive to this issue, the lack of appropriate instruction within the regular classroom may create concern.

Apprehension over delivery of appropriate services means that parents will often seek other educational options if the local school district is unable to serve the needs of their gifted child. One such option is to seek the above mentioned transfer to an adjoining public school district. As stated earlier, at one time transfers were relatively easy to obtain. However, in the last few years school districts have been reluctant to approve shifts across district lines. This reluctance stems from two very important administrative considerations. Many school districts are facing a financial crisis and are reluctant to forfeit any student generated attendance funding. Second, many school districts are operating under a school desegregation court order and student transfers become immediately suspect. Parents will continue to plead for such relief, but transfers will probably be granted by court order only in extraordinary cases.

A second option for the dissatisfied parent is to enroll the child in a private or parochial school. Because parents often want to maximize the abilities of their gifted child, it is extremely important that they carefully check to see that the private institution is operating as advertised. Is the curriculum congruent with the schedule of study presented in the printed promotional materials? Do the educational backgrounds of the teachers qualify them to teach gifted children? Are the teachers certified in the state? For the sake of their children and their financial resources, parents must be certain that no educational misrepresentation is taking place. At least one case of alleged fraud, deception, and misrepresentation is currently being litigated in Louisiana. Of course, misrepresentation may occur in the public schools as well. Whether the school is public or private, parents must be vigilant to see that administrators are abiding by state guidelines, laws, and school board policy in administering a gifted program. They should also read materials describing screening and identification, goals and objectives of the program, and how these are evaluated. It is up to parents to seek accountability in the education of their gifted and talented children.

Parents may wish to elect a third option, home schooling. For several different reasons, many parents who have lost confidence in the public, private, and parochial schools are attempting to educate their children at home. One legal issue arising from such situations involving the gifted includes: whether a parent may educate the child at home in the basic subjects but send the child to a public school gifted program. For example, if the school district operated a resource program 150 minutes a week, should the child being home schooled have access to that program? If the child may participate, should the district provide transportation for the home-schooled child if the district is busing students from other schools to a gifted program taught at a central location? If the administration is receiving money from the state to educate gifted children in that district, should the gifted child who is being completely taught at home receive a per capita share of these funds?

Due Process

As mentioned in Chapter Seven, due process hearings provide several points for future conflict. Practices in the selection of hearing officers vary and concerns arise when a person presiding over a hearing is affiliated with a public school, college, or university having a direct or indirect interest in the outcome. In many states, the gifted education field is composed of a small body of professionals who have constant contact with others in the discipline through professional meetings, research, educational offerings, and policy making. Therefore, a network often exists in the gifted education field within the states, and parents should be alert to partiality on the part of the hearing officer.

In this age of accountability, parents will also be interested in the qualifications and training of the hearing officer. Using a sports analogy, it would be difficult for a referee at a sporting event to effectively fulfill his or her responsibilities without knowing the objectives and the rules of the game. No less should be expected of a hearing officer making a decision involving a child's educational future. Because courts most often defer to the expert in the field, in this case the hearing officer, the impartiality, education, and training of a hearing officer is of particular importance to parents and school officials.

Tort Liability

While there are no data to suggest that gifted children are injured more frequently in accidents than other children, their innate curiosity, creativity, and participation in a variety of programs, including those in residential settings, possibly place them at risk. Because they usually function physically and socially at their chronological age and intellectually at a much higher level, this disparity strongly suggests that all staff members involved in gifted education should be extraordinarily vigilant. Field trips, experimental projects, travel to off-campus courses, dormitory living, and recreational activities can be hazardous to the gifted who are exceptionally curious and are thus prone to explore and test limits. Cases continue to arise in this area and courts are still establishing a body of jurisprudence regarding the liability of directors, teachers, and others. In order to better understand their legal responsibilities, all personnel with responsibility for supervision of gifted children and youth should be informed on basic tort liability and the scope of insurance protection.

Protecting a National Treasure

When future claims arise based on race, color, national origin, sex, handicap, or age, the Office for Civil Rights will continue to be a vital force in obtaining school district and state education agency compliance with federal laws (See Appendix D). The office has investigated alleged claims of racial discrimination in the screening and identification of children and youth for specialized programs for the gifted and the discrimination against handicapped in admission to gifted programs.

Should parents face an intractable gifted education problem, they might wish to contact the local American Civil Liberties Union office. The ACLU has an ongoing children's project and is particularly interested in federal constitutional violations such as race and gender discrimination, and freedom of speech and religion issues (See Appendix E).

A common and often used phrase, and one particularly stated at commencement time, is that today's young persons are one of America's great future resources. To make certain this phrase becomes a reality, the nation must expand the intellectual and creative abilities of its most gifted and talented young people. The legal system has been used to aid persons of all races, gender, nationalities, religions, and handicapping conditions to have the opportunity to develop their intellectual skills and talents to create a better life for themselves and their families. There is no doubt that in the future, legal alternatives, mediation, due process, and litigation will be utilized to provide protection for another identifiable minority — the gifted and talented. Until the protections are in place to allow these children the opportunity to fully maximize their abilities, America is leaving undeveloped one of its national treasures.

Table of Cases

In re Marriage of Mitchell, 103 Ill. App. 3d 242, 430 N.E. 2d 716 (1982)
Patrick v. Perfect Parts Co., 515 S.W. 2d 554 (Mo. 1974)
Powell v. Orleans Parish School Board, 354 So. 2d 229 (La. App. 1978)
Roe v. Commonwealth Department of Education, 638 F. Supp. 929 (E.D. Pa. 1987)
Rohn v. Thuma, 408 N.E. 2d 578 (Ind. App. 1980)
Rosen v. Montgomery City Intermediate Unit No. 23, 495 A. 2d 217 (Pa. Commw. Ct. 1985)
Rosenthal v. Orleans Parish School Board, 214 So. 2d 203 (La. App. 1968)
Sands Point Academy v. Board of Education, 311 N.Y.S. 2d 588 (1970)
Scott v. Commonwealth Department of Education, 512 A. 2d 790 (Pa. Commw. Ct. 1986)
Shestach v. General Braddock Area School District, 437 A. 2d 1059 (Pa. Commw. Ct. 1981)
Terveer v. Baschnagel, 445 N.E. 2d 264 (Ohio App. 1982)
Vaughns v. Board of Education of Prince George's County, 574 F. Supp. 1280; 758 F. 2d 983 (4th Cir. 1985)
Vorchheimer v. School District of Philadelphia, 532 F. 2d 880 (3rd Cir. 1976)
Wall v. American Employers Insurance Company, 377 So. 2d 369 (La. App. 1980)
Wallace v. State Industrial Court, 406 P. 2d 488 (Okla. 1965)
Wishart v. Andress, 361 N.Y.S. 2d 791 (1974)
Woodland Hills School v. Commonwealth Department of Education, 516 A. 2d 875 (Pa. Commw. Ct. 1986)
Zweifel v. Joint District No. 1, Belleville, 251 N.W. 2d 822 (Wisc. 1977)

Appendix A

Part B, Jacob K. Javits Gifted and Talented Students Education Act of 1988

"PART B — GIFTED AND TALENTED CHILDREN

"SEC.4101. SHORT TITLE.

"This part may be referred to as the 'Jacob K. Javits Gifted and Talented Students Education Act of 1988.'

"SEC.4012. FINDINGS AND PURPOSES.

"(a) FINDINGS — The Congress finds and declares that —

"(1) gifted and talented students are a national resource vital to the future of the Nation and its security and well-being;

"(2) unless the special abilities of gifted and talented students are recognized and developed during their elementary and secondary school years, much of their special potential for contributing to the national interest is likely to be lost;

"(3) gifted and talented students from economically disadvantaged families and areas, and students of limited English proficiency are at greatest risk of being unrecognized and of not being provided adequate or appropriate educational services;

"(4) State and local educational agencies and private nonprofit schools often lack the necessary specialized resources to plan and implement effective programs for the early identification of gifted and talented students for the provision of educational services and programs appropriate to their special needs; and

"(5) the Federal Government can best carry out the limited but essential role of stimulating research and development and personnel training, and providing a national focal point of information and technical assistance, that is necessary to ensure that our Nation's schools are able to meet the special educational needs of gifted and talented students, and thereby serve a profound national interest.

"(b) STATEMENT OF PURPOSE. It is the purpose of this part to provide financial assistance to State and local educational agencies, institutions of higher education, and other public and private agencies and organizations, to initiate a coordinated program of research, demonstration projects, personnel training, and similar activities designed to build a nationwide capability in elementary and secondary schools to identify and meet the special educational needs of gifted and talented students. It is also the purpose of this part to supplement and make more effective the expenditure of State and local funds, and of Federal funds made available under chapter 2 of title I of this Act and title II of this Act, for the education of gifted and talented students.

"SEC.4103.   DEFINITIONS.

"For the purposes of this part:

"(1) The term 'gifted and talented students' means children and youth who give evidence of high performance capability in areas such as intellectual, creative, artistic, or leadership capacity, or in specific academic fields, and who require services or activities not ordinarily provided by the school in order to fully develop such capabilities.

"(2) The term 'institution of higher education' has the same meaning given such term in section 435(b) of the Higher Education Act of 1965.

"(3) The term 'Hawaiian native' means any individual of whose ancestors were native prior to 1778 of the area which now comprises the State of Hawaii.

"(4) The term 'Hawaiian native organization' means any organization recognized by the Governor of the State of Hawaii primarily serving and representing Hawaiian natives.

"SEC.4104   AUTHORIZED PROGRAMS.

"(a) ESTABLISHMENT OF PROGRAM. From the sums appropriated under section 4108 in any fiscal year the Secretary (after consultation with experts in the field of the education of gifted and talented students) shall make grants to or enter into contracts with State educational agencies, local educational agencies, institutions of higher education, or other public agencies and private agencies and organizations (including Indian tribes and organizations as defined by the Indian Self-Determination and Education Assistance Act and Hawaiian native organizations) to assist such agencies, institutions, and organizations which submit applications in carrying out programs of projects authorized by this Act that are designed to meet the educational needs of gifted and talented students, including the training of personnel in the education of gifted and talented students or in supervising such personnel.

"(b) USES OF FUNDS. Programs and projects assisted under this section may include —

"(1) preservice and inservice training (including fellowships) for personnel (including leadership personnel) involved in the education of gifted and talented students;

"(2) establishment and operation of model projects and exemplary programs for the identification and education of gifted and talented students, including summer programs and cooperative programs involving business, industry, and education;

"(3) strengthening the capability of State educational agencies and institutions of higher education to provide leadership and assistance to local educational agencies and nonprofit private schools in the planning, operation, and improvement of programs for the identification and education of gifted and talented students;

"(4) programs of technical assistance and information dissemination; and

"(5) carrying out (through the National Center for Research and Development in the Education of Gifted and Talented Children and Youth established pursuant to subsection [c]) —

"(A) research on methods and techniques for identifying and teaching gifted and talented students, and

"(B) program evaluations, surveys, and the collection, analysis, and development of information needed to accomplish the purposes of this part.

"(c) ESTABLISHMENT OF NATIONAL CENTER. The Secretary (after consultation with experts in the field of the education of gifted and talented students) shall establish a National Center for Research and Development in the Education of Gifted and Talented Children and Youth through grants to or contracts with one or more institutions of higher education or State educational agencies, or a combination or consortium of such institutions and agencies, for the purpose of carrying out clause (5) of subsection (b). Such National Center shall have a Director. The Secretary may authorize the Director to carry out such functions of the National Center as may be agreed upon through arrangements with other institutions of higher education, State or local educational agencies, or other public or private agencies and organizations.

"(d) LIMITATION. Not more than 30 percent of the funds available in any fiscal year to carry out the programs and projects authorized by this section may be used for the conduct of activities pursuant to subsections (b)(5) or (c).

"SEC.4105. PROGRAM PRIORITIES.

"(a) GENERAL PRIORITY. In the administration of this part the Secretary shall give highest priority —

"(1) to the identification of gifted and talented students who may not be identified through traditional assessment methods (including economically disadvantaged individuals, individuals of limited English proficiency, and individuals with handicaps) and to education programs designed to include gifted and talented students from such groups; and

"(2) to programs and projects designed to develop or improve the capability of schools in an entire State or region of the Nation through cooperative efforts and participation of State and local educational agencies, institutions of higher education, and other public and private agencies and organizations (including business, industry, and labor), to plan, conduct, and improve programs for the identification and education of gifted and talented students.

"(b) SERVICE PRIORITY. In approving applications under section 4104(a) of this part, the Secretary shall assure that in each fiscal year at least one-half of the applications approved contain a component designed to serve gifted and talented students who are economically disadvantaged individuals.

"SEC.4106. PARTICIPATION OF PRIVATE SCHOOL CHILDREN AND TEACHERS.

"In making grants and entering into contracts under this Act, the Secretary shall ensure, where appropriate, that provision is made for the equitable participation of students and teachers in private nonprofit elementary and secondary schools, including the participation of teachers and other personnel in preservice and inservice training programs for serving such children.

"SEC.4107. ADMINISTRATION.

"The Secretary shall establish or designate an administrative unit within the Department of Education —

"(1) to administer the program authorized by this part,

"(2) to coordinate all programs for gifted and talented students administered by the Department, and

"(3) to serve as a focal point of national leadership and information on the educational needs of gifted and talented students and the availability of educational services and programs designed to meet those needs.

The administrative unit established or designated pursuant to this section shall be headed by a person of recognized professional qualifications and experience in the field of the education of gifted and talented students.

"SEC.4108. AUTHORIZATION OF APPROPRIATIONS.

"There are authorized to be appropriated $20,000,000 for the fiscal year 1989 and such sums as may be necessary for each of the fiscal years 1990, 1991, 1992, and 1993, to carry out the provisions of this part.

Appendix B

State Bar Associations

Alabama

Alabama State Bar
P.O. Box 671
Montgomery, AL 36101

Alaska

Alaska Bar Association
P.O. Box 100279
Anchorage, AK 99510

Arizona

State Bar of Arizona
363 N. 1st Ave.
Phoenix, AZ 85003

Arkansas

Arkansas Bar Association
400 W. Markham
Little Rock, AR 72201

California

State Bar of California
555 Franklin St.
San Francisco, CA 94012

Colorado

The Colorado Bar Association
1900 Grant St. #950
Denver, CO 80203

Connecticut

Connecticut Bar Association
101 Corporate Place
Rocky Hill, CT 06067

Delaware

Delaware State Bar Association
P.O. Box 1709
Wilmington, DE 19899

District of Columbia

The District of Columbia Bar
1707 L St. NW, 6th Floor
Washington, DC 20036

Bar Association of the
    District of Columbia
1819 H St. NW, 12th Floor
Washington, DC 20006

Florida

The Florida Bar
650 Apalachee Parkway
Tallahassee, FL 32399

Georgia

State Bar of Georgia
800 The Hurt Bldg.
Atlanta, GA 30303

Hawaii

Hawaii State Bar Association
P.O. Box 26
Honolulu, HI 96810

Idaho

Idaho State Bar
P.O. Box 895
Boise, ID 83701

Illinois

Illinois State Bar Association
424 S. Second St.
Springfield, IL 62701

Indiana

Indiana State Bar Association
230 E. Ohio, 6th Floor
Indianapolis, IN 46204

Iowa

Iowa State Bar Association
1101 Fleming Bldg.
Des Moines, IA 50309

Kansas

Kansas Bar Association
P.O. Box 1037
Topeka, KS 66601

Kentucky

Kentucky Bar Association
West Main at Kentucky River
Frankfort, KY 40601

Louisiana

Louisiana State Bar Association
601 St. Charles Ave.
New Orleans, LA 70130

Maine

Maine State Bar Association
P.O. Box 788
Augusta, ME 04332-0788

Maryland

Maryland State Bar Association
520 W. Fayette St.
Baltimore, MD 21201

Massachusetts

Massachusetts Bar Association
20 West St.
Boston, MA 02111

Michigan

State Bar of Michigan
306 Townsend St.
Lansing, MI 48933-2083

Minnesota

Minnesota State Bar Association
430 Marquette Ave., Suite 403
Minneapolis, MN 55401

Mississippi

Mississippi State Bar
P.O. Box 2168
Jackson, MS 39225-2168

Missouri

The Missouri Bar
P.O. Box 119
Jefferson City, MO 65102

Montana

State Bar of Montana
P.O. Box 577
Helena, MT 59624

Nebraska

Nebraska State Bar Association
P.O. Box 81809
Lincoln, NE 68501

Nevada

State Bar of Nevada
500 S. 3rd St. #2
Las Vegas, NV 89101-1085

New Hampshire

New Hampshire Bar Association
112 Pleasant St.
Concord, NH 03301

New Jersey

New Jersey State Bar Association
One Constitution Square
New Brunswick, NJ 08901-1500

New Mexico

State Bar of New Mexico
P.O. Box 25883
Albuquerque, NM 87125

New York

New York State Bar Association
One Elk St.
Albany, NY 12207

North Carolina

North Carolina State Bar
P.O. Box 25908
Raleigh, NC 27611

North Carolina Bar Association
P.O. Box 12806
Raleigh, NC 27605

North Dakota

State Bar Association of
    North Dakota
515½ E. Broadway, Suite 101
Bismarck, ND 58501

Ohio

Ohio State Bar Association
33 W. Eleventh Ave.
Columbus, OH 43201

Oklahoma

Oklahoma Bar Association
P.O. Box 53036
Oklahoma City, OK 73152

Oregon

Oregon State Bar
P.O. Box 1689
Lake Oswego, OR 97035

Pennsylvania

Pennsylvania Bar Association
P.O. Box 186
Harrisburg, PA 17108

Puerto Rico

Puerto Rico Bar Association
P.O. Box 1900
San Juan, PR 00903

Rhode Island

Rhode Island Bar Association
91 Friendship St.
Providence, RI 02903

South Carolina

South Carolina Bar
P.O. Box 608
Columbia, SC 29202

South Dakota

State Bar of South Dakota
222 E. Capitol
Pierre, SD 57501

Tennessee

Tennessee Bar Association
3622 West End Ave.
Nashville, TN 37205

Texas

State Bar of Texas
P.O. Box 12487
Austin, TX 78711

Utah

Utah State Bar
645 S. 200 East
Salt Lake City, UT 84111

Vermont

Vermont Bar Association
P.O. Box 100
Montpelier, VT 05601

Virginia

Virginia State Bar
801 E. Main St.
Ross Bldg., Suite 1000
Richmond, VA 23219

Virginia Bar Association
7th & Franklin Bldg.
701 E. Franklin St. #1515
Richmond, VA 23219

Virgin Islands

Virgin Islands Bar Association
P.O. Box 4108
Christiansted, VI 00822

Washington

Washington State Bar
    Association
500 Westin Bldg.
2001 Sixth Ave.
Seattle, WA 98121-2599

West Virginia

West Virginia State Bar
E-400 State Capitol
Charleston, WV 25305

West Virginia Bar Association
P.O. Box 346
Charleston, WV 25322

Wisconsin

State Bar of Wisconsin
402 W. Wilson
Madison, WI 53703

Wyoming

Wyoming State Bar
P.O. Box 109
Cheyenne, WY 82003-0109

Appendix C

National and International
Professional Associations and Advocacy Groups
for Gifted Children and Adults

American Association for Gifted Children
Talent Identification Program
Duke University
Box 40077
Durham, NC 27706-0077

This association has research as the primary focus. It strives to supplement similar organizations in gifted education.

American Mensa, Ltd.
2626 East 14th Street
Brooklyn, NY 11235-3992

Mensa is an organization for highly intelligent persons; membership is determined on a standardized intelligence test score higher than 98 percent of the general population. The organization sponsors meetings and publications.

The Association for the Gifted (TAG)
Council for Exceptional Children
1920 Association Drive
Reston, VA 22091

This association is a division of the Council for Exceptional Children. Publications include books, a journal, and a newsletter. They are involved in legislative activity on behalf of gifted children.

The Council of State Directors of Programs for Gifted
G/T Programs Consultant
Maine Dept. of Education
     and Cultural Services
State House Station #23
Augusta, ME 04333

The Council is composed of state directors of gifted and talented programs. Their primary focus is the development and dissemination of current information on gifted education across the United States. They published *The 1987 State of the States Gifted and Talented Education Report;* an updated report is scheduled to be issued in 1991.

Gifted Child Society, Inc.
190 Rock Road
Glen Rock, NJ 07452

The society was founded to further the cause of gifted education through educational and support services for the gifted. Special programs and services are also available for their parents and other adults.

The Institute for Law and Gifted Education
909 South 34th Avenue
Hattiesburg, MS 39402

The Institute serves as a clearinghouse for legal issues involving gifted students. Workshops, seminars, and consultations are provided.

The National Association for Creative Children and Adults
8080 Springvalley Drive
Cincinnati, OH 45236

This group focuses on the development and nurturing of creativity in children and adults.

National Association for Gifted Children (NAGC)
1155 15th Street NW
Suite 1002
Washington, DC 20005

The association publishes a journal and a newsletter, as well as other materials in gifted education for the membership composed of professionals and parents. Also conducts an annual convention. The association is active in promoting legislation.

National/State Leadership Training Institute
  on the Gifted and Talented
316 West Second Street
Suite PH C
Los Angeles, CA 90012

Parents, educators, and administrators of the gifted are provided workshops and consultation by this group. In addition, they publish many books and other printed materials.

Supporting Emotional Needs of Gifted (SENG)
School of Professional Psychology
Wright State University
P.O. Box 2745
Dayton, OH 45401

This association is dedicated to the emotional and social needs of the gifted. A variety of services are offered including an annual conference.

The World Council for Gifted and Talented Children, Inc.
Executive Secretary
College of Education
Lamar University
Beaumont, TX 77704

This association promoted the needs of the gifted and creative world wide. An international conference is conducted every two years.

Appendix D

US Department of Education
Office for Civil Rights
Regional Civil Rights Offices

Region I –   Connecticut, Maine, Massachusetts, New Hampshire, Rhode Island, Vermont

Regional Civil Rights Director
US Department of Education
Office for Civil Rights, Region I
John W. McCormack POCH
Post Office Square, Room 222
Boston, MA 02109

Region II –   New Jersey, New York, Puerto Rico, Virgin Islands

Regional Civil Rights Director
US Department of Education
Office for Civil Rights, Region II
26 Federal Plaza, 33rd Floor
New York, NY 10278

Region III –   Delaware, District of Columbia, Maryland, Pennsylvania, Virginia, West Virginia

Regional Civil Rights Director
US Department of Education
Office for Civil Rights, Region III
Gateway Building, 3535 Market Street
Room 6300
Philadelphia, PA 19104-3326

Region IV –   Alabama, Florida, Georgia, Kentucky, Mississippi, North Carolina, South Carolina, Tennessee

Regional Civil Rights Director
US Department of Education
Office for Civil Rights, Region IV
101 Marietta Tower, 27th Floor
P.O. Box 1705
Atlanta, GA 30301

Region V –   Illinois, Indiana, Minnesota, Michigan, Ohio, Wisconsin

Regional Civil Rights Director
US Department of Education
Office for Civil Rights, Region V
401 South State Street, 7th Floor
Chicago, IL 60605

Region VI –   Arkansas, Louisiana, New Mexico, Oklahoma, Texas

Regional Civil Rights Director
US Department of Education
Office for Civil Rights, Region VI
1200 Main Tower Building, Suite 2260
Dallas, TX 75202

Region VII –   Iowa, Kansas, Missouri, Nebraska

Regional Civil Rights Director
US Department of Education
Office for Civil Rights, Region VII
P.O. Box 901381
10220 N. Executive Hills Blvd.
8th Floor
Kansas City, MO 64190-1381

Region VIII – Colorado, Montana, North Dakota, South Dakota, Utah,
               Wyoming

Regional Civil Rights Director
US Department of Education
Office for Civil Rights, Region VIII
1961 Stout Street, Room 342
Denver, CO 80294

Region IX –   Arizona, California, Hawaii, Nevada, Guam, Trust Territory
               of the Pacific Islands, American Samoa

Regional Civil Rights Director
US Department of Education
Office for Civil Rights
Region IX
221 Main Street, 10th Floor
San Francisco, CA 94105

Region X –   Alaska, Idaho, Oregon, Washington

Regional Civil Rights Director
US Department of Education
Office for Civil Rights, Region X
2901 3rd Avenue, Room 100
Seattle, WA 98121-1042

Appendix E

The American Civil Liberties Union Offices

American Civil Liberties Union
132 West 43rd Street
New York, NY 10036

**ACLU National Legislative
    Office**
600 Pennsylvania Avenue SE
Washington, DC 20003

**ACLU Mountain States Regional
    Office**
2160 South Holly
Denver, CO 80222

ACLU Southern Regional Office
52 Fairlie Street NW
Atlanta, GA 30303

National Prison Project
1346 Connecticut Avenue NW
Washington, DC 20036

**Center for National Security
    Studies**
122 Maryland Avenue NE
Washington, DC 20002

Alabama CLU
P.O. Box 447
Montgomery, AL 36101

Alaska CLU
P.O. Box 11-1226
Anchorage, AK 99511

Arizona CLU
1433 North 1st Street
Phoenix, AZ 85004

ACLU of Arkansas
P.O. Box 2832
Little Rock, AR 72203

ACLU of No. California
1663 Mission Street
San Francisco, CA 94103

ACLU of So. California
633 South Shatto Place
Los Angeles, CA 90005

ACLU of Colorado
815 E. 22nd Avenue
Denver, CO 80205

Connecticut CLU
22 Maple Avenue
Hartford, CT 06114

ACLU of Delaware
903 French Street
Wilmington, DE 19801

ACLU of Florida
7210 South Red Road
South Miami, FL 33143

ACLU of Georgia
88 Walton Street NW
Atlanta, GA 30303

ACLU of Hawaii
217 South King Street
Honolulu, HI 96813

ACLU of Illinois
220 South State Street
Chicago, IL 60604

Indiana CLU
445 North Pennsylvania St.
Indianapolis, IN 46204

Iowa CLU
102 E. Grand Avenue
Des Moines, IA 50309

ACLU of Kansas
8001 Conser
Overland Park, KS 66204

Kentucky CLU
809 South Fourth Street
Louisville, KY 40203

ACLU of Louisiana
348 Baronne Street
New Orleans, LA 70112

Maine CLU
97A Exchange Street
Portland, ME 04101

ACLU of Maryland
744 Dulaney Valley Court
Towson, MD 21204

ACLU of Massachusetts
47 Winter Street
Boston, MA 02108

ACLU of Michigan
1553 Woodward Avenue
Detroit, MI 48226

Minnesota CLU
628 Central Avenue
Minneapolis, MN 55414

ACLU of Mississippi
528 North State Street
Jackson, MS 39201

ACLU of Eastern Missouri
4557 Laclede Avenue
St. Louis, MO 63108

ACLU of Western Missouri
8001 Conser
Overland Park, KS 66204

ACLU of Montana
P.O. Box 3012
Billings, MT 59103

Nebraska CLU
Box 81455
Lincoln, NE 68501

ACLU of Nevada
135 North Sierra
Reno, NV 89501

New Hampshire CLU
11 South Main
Concord, NH 03301

ACLU of New Jersey
38 Walnut Street
Newark, NJ 07102

ACLU of New Mexico
1803 Carlisle NE
Albuquerque, NM 87110

New York CLU
84 Fifth Avenue
New York, NY 10011

North Carolina CLU
P.O. Box 3094
Greensboro, NC 27402

ACLU of Ohio
360 South Third Street
Columbus, OH 43215-5463

ACLU of Oklahoma
P.O. Box 799
Oklahoma City, OK 73101

ACLU of Oregon
310 SW Fourth Avenue
Portland, OR 97204

ACLU of Pennsylvania
1324 Walnut Street
Philadelphia, PA 19107

ACLU of Greater Philadelphia
1324 Walnut Street
Philadelphia, PA 19107

Rhode Island CLU
212 Union Street
Providence, RI 02903

ACLU of South Carolina
533-B Harden Street
Columbia, SC 29205

ACLU of Tennessee
P.O. Box 120160
Nashville, TN 37212

Texas CLU
600 West Seventh Street
Austin, TX 78701

ACLU of Utah
8 East Broadway
Salt Lake City, UT 84111

ACLU of Vermont
43 State Street
Montpelier, VT 05602

ACLU of Virginia
112A North 7th Street
Richmond, VA 23219

ACLU of Washington
Smith Tower
Seattle, WA 98104

ACLU of the National Capital Area
600 Pennsylvania Avenue SE
Washington, DC 20003

West Virginia CLU
P.O. Box 1509
Charleston, WV 25325

Wisconsin CLU
207 E. Buffalo Street
Milwaukee, WI 53202

Appendix F

State Consultants in Gifted Education

Alabama

Program for Exceptional Children
Alabama State Dept. of Education
1020 Monticello Court
Montgomery, AL 36117

Alaska

Gifted and Talented Education
Department of Special Services
P.O. Box F
Juneau, AK 99811-9981

American Samoa

Gifted/Talented Education
American Samoa Dept. of
    Education
Pago Pago, AS 96799

Arizona

Arizona Department of Education
1535 West Jefferson
Phoenix, AZ 85007

Arkansas

Programs for Gifted/Talented
Room 105-C, Education Building
4 Capitol Mall
Little Rock, AK 72201

California

Gifted and Talented Education
California Dept. of Education
P.O. Box 944272
Sacramento, CA 94244-2720

Colorado

Gifted and Talented Education
Colorado Dept. of Education
201 East Colfax
Denver, CO 80203

Connecticut

Gifted/Talented Programs
Connecticut Dept. of Education
25 Industrial Park Road
Middletown, CT 06457

Delaware

Gifted and Talented Programs
Delaware Dept. of Instruction
P.O. Box 1402, Townsend Building
Dover, DE 19903

District of Columbia

Gifted/Talented Education Program
Nalle School, 50th and C Street SE
Washington, DC 20019

Florida

Gifted Program
Bureau of Exceptional Children
Florida Dept. of Education
654 Florida Education Centre
Tallahassee, FL 32399-0400

Georgia

Gifted Education
Division of General Instruction
Georgia Dept. of Education
1952 Twin Towers East
Atlanta, GA 30334-5040

Guam

GATE
Department of Education
P.O. Box DE
Agana, GU 96910

Hawaii

Gifted and Talented
Office of Instructional Services
189 Lunalilo Home Road
Honolulu, HI 96825

Idaho

Idaho Department of Education
Len B. Jordan Office Building
650 West State
Boise, ID 83720

Illinois

Curriculum Improvement Section
  N-242
Illinois Board of Education
100 North First Street
Springfield, IL 62777

Indiana

Gifted and Talented
Indiana Dept. of Education
229 State House
Indianapolis, IN 46204

Iowa

Gifted Education
Department of Education
Grimes State Office Building
Des Moines, IA 50319-0146

Kansas

Gifted/Talented Education
Kansas Dept. of Education
120 East 10th
Topeka, KS 66612

Kentucky

Gifted/Talented Education
Kentucky Dept. of Education
1831 Capitol Plaza Tower
Frankfort, KY 40601

Louisiana

Gifted/Talented Programs
Louisiana Dept. of Education
P.O. Box 94064
Baton Rouge, LA 70804-9064

Maine

Gifted/Talented Programs
Maine Dept. of Education
  and Cultural Services
State House Station #23
Augusta, ME 04333

Maryland

Gifted/Talented Division
Maryland Dept. of Education
200 W. Baltimore Street
Baltimore, MD 21201

Massachusetts

Gifted/Talented
Bureau of Curriculum Service
Massachusetts Dept. of
  Education
1385 Hancock St.
Quincy, MA 02169

Michigan

Gifted and Talented
Michigan Dept. of Education
P.O. Box 30008
Lansing, MI 48909

Minnesota
Gifted Education
Minnesota Dept. of Education
550 Cedar Street
St. Paul, MN 55101

Mississippi
Gifted and Talented
Bureau of Special Service
Mississippi Dept. of Education
P.O. Box 771
Jackson, MS 39205-0771

Missouri
Gifted Education
Missouri Dept. of Elementary
  and Secondary Education
P.O. Box 480
100 East Capitol
Jefferson City, MO 65102

Montana
Gifted/Talented
Office of Public Instruction
State Capitol
Helena, MT 59620

Nebraska
Gifted/Talented Program
Nebraska Dept. of Education
P.O. Box 94987
300 Centennial Mall South
Lincoln, NE 68509

Nevada
Gifted/Talented Program
Special Education Branch
Nevada Dept. of Education
400 West King Street
Capitol Complex
Carson City, NV 89710

New Hampshire
Gifted Education
New Hampshire Dept. of Education
101 Pleasant Street
Concord, NH 03301

New Jersey
Gifted and Talented
Division of General Academic
  Education
New Jersey Dept. of Education
225 W. State Street, CN 500
Trenton, NJ 08625-0500

New Mexico
Gifted/Talented Special Education
Education Building
Santa Fe, NM 87501-2786

New York
Gifted Education
New York Dept. of Education
Room 212 EB
Albany, NY 12234

North Carolina
Gifted Education
Division for Exceptional Children
North Carolina Dept. of Public
  Instruction
116 W. Edenton Street
Education Building
Raleigh, NC 27603-1712

North Dakota
Gifted and Talented Education
North Dakota Dept. of
  Public Instruction
State Capitol
Bismarck, ND 58505

Ohio

Gifted Education
Ohio Division of Special Education
933 High Street
Worthington, OH 43085

Oklahoma

Gifted and Talented Section
Oklahoma Dept. of Education
2500 N. Lincoln Blvd.
Oklahoma City, OK 73105

Oregon

Gifted and Talented Specialist
700 Pringle Parkway SE
Salem, OR 97219

Pennsylvania

Gifted and Talented
Bureau of Special Education
Pennsylvania Dept. of Education
333 Market Street
Harrisburg, PA 17126-0333

Puerto Rico

Gifted Education
Puerto Rico Dept. of Education
Office of External Resources
Hato Rey, PR 00924

Rhode Island

Gifted and Talented Education
Department of Elementary and
    Secondary Education
22 Hayes Street
Providence, RI 02908

South Carolina

Gifted Program
802 Rutledge Bldg., 1429 Senate St.
Columbia, SC 29201

South Dakota

Gifted Programs
Special Education Section
South Dakota Dept. of Education
700 North Illinois
Richard F. Kneip Building
Pierre, SD 57501

Tennessee

Gifted and Talented Programs and
    Services
Tennessee Dept. of Education
132-A Cordell Hull Building
Nashville, TN 37219

Texas

Gifted and Talented
Texas Education Agency
1701 N. Congress Avenue
Austin, TX 78701

Trust Territory

Federal Programs Coordinator
Office of Special Education
Trust Territory Office of Education
Office of the High Commissioner
Saipan, CM 96950

Utah

Gifted and Talented Education
Utah Dept. of Education
250 E. 500 South
Salt Lake City, UT 84111

Vermont

Gifted Education
Vermont Dept. of Education
Montpelier, VT 05602

Virgin Islands

Gifted/Talented Education
St. Thomas/St. John School
    District
#44-46 Kongens Gade
St. Thomas, VI 00802

Virginia

Gifted Programs
Virginia Dept. of Education
P.O. Box 6-Q
Richmond, VA 23216-2060

Washington

Gifted Programs
Superintendent of Public
    Instruction
Old Capitol Building FG-11
Olympia, WA 98504

West Virginia

Gifted Programs
Office of Special Education
West Virginia Dept. of Education
Capitol Building 6, Room B-304
Charleston, WV 25305

Wisconsin

Gifted and Talented Program
Wisconsin Dept. of Public
    Instruction
P.O. Box 7841, 125 S. Webster
Madison, WI 53707

Wyoming

Language Arts, Gifted and Talented
Wyoming Dept. of Education
Hathaway Building
Cheyenne, WY 82002

Appendix G

The Attorneys General of the States
and Other Jurisdictions

Alabama

Attorney General of Alabama
South House
11 South Union Street
Montgomery, AL 36130

Alaska

Attorney General of Alaska
P.O. Box K. State Capitol
Juneau, AK 99811-0300

American Samoa

Attorney General of
    American Samoa
P.O. Box 7
Pago Pago, AS 96799

Arizona

Attorney General of Arizona
1275 West Washington
Phoenix, AZ 85007

Arkansas

Attorney General of Arkansas
200 Tower Building
4th and Center Streets
Little Rock, AK 72201

California

Attorney General of California
1515 K Street, Suite 638
Sacramento, CA 95814

Colorado

Attorney General of Colorado
1525 Sherman Street, Second Floor
Denver, CO 80203

Connecticut

Attorney General of Connecticut
55 Elm Street
Hartford, CT 06106

Delaware

Attorney General of Delaware
820 North French Street
8th Floor
Wilmington, DE 19801

District of Columbia

Corporate Counsel of the
    District of Columbia
1350 Pennsylvania Avenue NW
Suite 329
Washington, DC 20004

Florida

Attorney General of Florida
State Capitol
Tallahassee, FL 32399-1050

Georgia

Attorney General of Georgia
132 State Judicial Building
Atlanta, GA 30334

Guam

Department of Law
238 F.C. Flores Street, #701
Agana, GU 96910

Hawaii

Attorney General of Hawaii
State Capitol, Room 405
Honolulu, HI 96813

Idaho

Attorney General of Idaho
State House
Boise, ID 83720

Illinois

Attorney General of Illinois
100 W. Randolph Street
12th Floor
Chicago, IL 60601
        or
500 S. Second Street
Springfield, IL 62706

Indiana

Attorney General of Indiana
219 State House
Indianapolis, IN 46204

Iowa

Attorney General of Iowa
Hoover Building, Second Floor
Des Moines, IA 50319

Kansas

Attorney General of Kansas
Judicial Center
Second Floor
Topeka, KS 66612

Kentucky

Attorney General of Kentucky
State Capitol
Room 116
Frankfort, KY 40601

Louisiana

Attorney General of Louisiana
2-3-4 Loyla Building
New Orleans, LA 70112
        or
P.O. Box 94005
Baton Rouge, LA 70804-9005

Maine

Attorney General of Maine
State House
Augusta, ME 04330

Maryland

Attorney General of Maryland
200 St. Paul Place
Baltimore, MD 21202

Massachusetts

Attorney General of Massachusetts
One Ashburton Place
20th Floor
Boston, MA 02108

Michigan

Attorney General of Michigan
Law Building
Lansing, MI 48913

Minnesota

Attorney General of Minnesota
102 State Capitol
St. Paul, MN 55155

Mississippi

Attorney General of Mississippi
P.O. Box 220
Jackson, MS 39205

Missouri

Attorney General of Missouri
Supreme Court Building
101 High Street
Jefferson City, MO 65102

Montana

Attorney General of Montana
Justice Building
215 North Sanders
Helena, MT 59620

Nebraska

Attorney General of Nebraska
2115 State Capitol
Lincoln, NE 68509

Nevada

Attorney General of Nevada
Heroes Memorial Building,
    Capitol Complex
Carson City, NV 89710

New Hampshire

Attorney General of
    New Hampshire
208 State House Annex
Concord, NH 03301

New Jersey

Attorney General of New Jersey
Richard J. Hughes Justice Complex
CN 080
Trenton, NJ 08625

New Mexico

Attorney General of New Mexico
Bataan Memorial Bldg.
Galisteo Street
Santa Fe, NM 87503-1508

New York

Attorney General of New York
120 Broadway, 25th Floor
New York NY 10271

North Carolina

Attorney General of North Carolina
Department of Justice
2 East Morgan Street
Raleigh, NC 27602

North Dakota

Attorney General of North Dakota
Department of Justice
2115 State Capitol
Bismarck, ND 58505

Northern Mariana Islands

Attorney General of the
    Commonwealth of the Northern
    Mariana Islands
Saipan, CM 96950

Ohio

Attorney General of Ohio
State Office Tower
30 E. Broad Street
Columbus, OH 43266-0410

Oklahoma

Attorney General of Oklahoma
112 State Capitol
Oklahoma City, OK 73105

Oregon

Attorney General of Oregon
100 Justice Building
Salem, OR 97310

Pennsylvania

Attorney General of Pennsylvania
Strawberry Square
16th Floor
Harrisburg, PA 17120

Puerto Rico

Attorney General of Puerto Rico
Department of Justice
P.O. Box 192
San Juan, PR 00902

Rhode Island

Attorney General of Rhode Island
72 Pine Street
Providence, RI 02903

South Carolina

Attorney General of South Carolina
Rembert Dennis Office Building
1000 Assembly Street
Columbia, SC 29211

South Dakota

Attorney General of South Dakota
State Capitol Building
Pierre, SD 57501

Tennessee

Attorney General of Tennessee
450 James Robertson Parkway
Nashville, TN 37219

Texas

Attorney General of Texas
P.O. Box 12548
Capitol Station
Austin, TX 78711

Utah

Attorney General of Utah
236 State Capitol
Salt Lake City, UT 84114

Vermont

Attorney General of Vermont
Pavilion Office Building
Montpelier, VT 05602

Virgin Islands

Attorney General of the
    Virgin Islands
Department of Justice
No. 48B-50C Kronprindsens Gade
G.E.R.S. Complex, 2nd Floor
Charlotte Amalie
St. Thomas, VI 00802

Virginia

Attorney General of Virginia
101 N. 8th Street, 5th Floor
Richmond, VA 23219

Washington

Attorney General of Washington
Highways-Licenses Building, PB 71
Olympia, WA 98504

West Virginia

Attorney General of West Virginia
State Capitol
Charleston, WV 25305

Wisconsin

Attorney General of Wisconsin
114 East, State Capitol
P.O. Box 7857
Madison, WI 53707-7857

Wyoming

Attorney General of Wyoming
123 State Capitol
Cheyenne, WY 82002

Appendix H

Chief State School Officers

Alabama

Superintendent of Education
State Dept. of Education
Gordon Persons Office Building
50 North Ripley Street
Montgomery, AL 36130-3901

Alaska

Commissioner of Education
State Dept. of Education
Alaska State Office Bldg., Pouch F
Juneau, AK 99811

American Samoa

Director of Education
Department of Education
Pago Pago, AS 96799

Arizona

Superintendent of Public
  Instruction
State Dept. of Education
1535 West Jefferson
Phoenix, AZ 85007

Arkansas

Director, General Education Div.
State Dept. of Education
Little Rock, AK 72201-1071

California

Superintendent of Public
  Instruction
State Dept. of Education
721 Capitol Mall
Sacramento, CA 95814

Colorado

Commissioner of Education
State Dept. of Education
201 East Colfax
Denver, CO 80203

Connecticut

Commissioner of Education
State Dept. of Education
165 Capitol Avenue
Room 308, State Office Bldg.
Hartford, CT 06106

Delaware

Superintendent of Public
  Instruction
State Dept. of Public Instruction
Townsend Building
P.O. Box 1402
Dover, DE 19901

District of Columbia

Superintendent of Public Schools
District of Columbia Public
  Schools
415 Twelfth Street NW
Washington, DC 20004

Florida

Commissioner of Education
State Dept. of Education
Capitol Building
Room PL 116
Tallahassee, FL 32399

Georgia

Superintendent of Schools
State Dept. of Education
2066 Twin Towers East
Atlanta, GA 30334

Guam

Director of Education
Department of Education
P.O. Box DE
Agana, GU 96910

Hawaii

Superintendent of Education
Department of Education
P.O. Box 2360
1390 Miller Street, #307
Honolulu, HI 96804

Idaho

Superintendent of Public
   Instruction
State Dept. of Education
650 West State Street
Boise, ID 83720

Illinois

Superintendent of Education
State Board of Education
100 North First Street
Springfield, IL 62777

Indiana

Superintendent of Public
   Instruction
State Dept. of Education
State House, Room 229
Indianapolis, IN 46204-2798

Iowa

Director of Education
State Dept. of Education
Grimes State Office Building
East 14th & Grand Streets
Des Moines, IA 50319-0146

Kansas

Commissioner of Education
State Dept. of Education
120 East Tenth Street
Topeka, KS 66612

Kentucky

Superintendent of Public
   Instruction
State Dept. of Education
1725 Capitol Plaza Tower
Frankfort, KY 40601

Louisiana

Superintendent of Education
State Dept. of Education
P.O. Box 94064
Baton Rouge, LA 70804-9064

Maine

Commissioner of Education
Dept. of Education and
   and Cultural Services
State House, Station #23
Augusta, ME 04333

Maryland

State Superintendent of Schools
State Dept. of Education
200 West Baltimore Street
Baltimore, MD 21201

Massachusetts
Commissioner of Education
State Dept. of Education
Quincy Center Plaza
1385 Hancock Street
Quincy, MA 02169

Michigan
Superintendent of Public
    Instruction
State Dept. of Education
P.O. Box 30008
608 West Allegan Street
Lansing, MI 48909

Minnesota
Commissioner of Education
State Dept. of Education
712 Capitol Square Building
550 Cedar Street
St. Paul, MN 55101

Mississippi
Superintendent of Education
State Dept. of Education
P.O. Box 771, High Street
Jackson, MS 39205-0771

Missouri
Commissioner of Education
Dept. of Elementary and
    Secondary Education
P.O. Box 480
205 Jefferson Street, 6th Floor
Jefferson City, MO 65102

Montana
Superintendent of Public
    Instruction
State Office of Public Instruction
106 State Capitol
Helena, MT 59620

Nebraska
Commissioner of Education
State Dept. of Education
P.O. Box 94987
301 Centennial Mall, South
Lincoln, NE 68509

Nevada
Superintendent of Public
    Instruction
State Dept. of Education
400 West King Street
Capitol Complex
Carson City, NV 89710

New Hampshire
Commissioner of Education
State Dept. of Education
101 Pleasant Street
State Office Park South
Concord, NH 03301

New Jersey
Commissioner of Education
State Dept. of Education
225 West State Street
Trenton, NJ 08625-0500

New Mexico
Superintendent of Public
    Instruction
State Dept. of Education Building
300 Don Gaspar
Santa Fe, NM 87501-2786

New York
Commissioner of Education
State Education Department
111 Education Building
Washington Avenue
Albany, NY 12234

North Carolina

Superintendent of Public
Instruction
State Dept. of Public Instruction
Education Building, Room 318
Edenton & Salisbury Streets
Raleigh, NC 27603-1712

North Dakota

Superintendent of Public
Instruction
State Dept. of Public Instruction
State Capitol Building
11th Floor
600 Blvd. Avenue East
Bismarck, ND 58505-0164

Northern Mariana Islands

Commissioner of Education
Commonwealth of the Northern
Mariana Islands
Department of Education
P.O. Box 1370 CK
Saipan, CM 96950

Ohio

Superintendent of Public
Instruction
State Dept. of Education
65 South Front Street, Room 808
Columbus, OH 43266-0308

Oklahoma

Superintendent of Public
Instruction
State Dept. of Education
Oliver Hodge Memorial Education
Building
2500 North Lincoln Blvd.
Oklahoma City, OK 73105-4599

Oregon

Superintendent of Public
Instruction
State Dept. of Education
700 Pringle Parkway SE
Salem, OR 97310

Pennsylvania

Acting Secretary of Education
State Dept. of Education
333 Market Street, 10th Floor
Harrisburg, PA 17126

Puerto Rico

Secretary of Education
Department of Education
P.O. Box 759
Hato Rey, PR 00919

Rhode Island

Commissioner of Education
State Dept. of Education
22 Hayes Street
Providence, RI 02908

South Carolina

State Superintendent of Education
State Dept. of Education
1006 Rutledge Building
1429 Senate Street
Columbia, SC 29201

South Dakota

State Superintendent
Dept. of Education and Cultural
Affairs
Div. of Elementary and Secondary
Education
700 Governors Drive
Pierre, SD 57501

Tennessee

Commissioner of Education
State Dept. of Education
100 Cordell Hull Building
Nashville, TN 37219

Texas

Commissioner of Education
Texas Education Agency
William B. Travis Building
1701 N. Congress Avenue
Austin, TX 78701-1494

Utah

Superintendent of Public
   Instruction
State Office of Education
250 East 500 South
Salt Lake City, UT 84111

Vermont

Commissioner of Education
State Dept. of Education
120 State Street
Montpelier, VT 05602-2703

Virginia

Superintendent of Public
   Instruction
State Dept. of Education
P.O. Box 6Q
James Monroe Building
Fourteenth & Franklin Streets
Richmond, VA 23216-2060

Virgin Islands

Commissioner of Education
Department of Education
44-46 Kongens Gade
St. Thomas, VI 00802

Washington

Superintendent of Public
   Instruction
State Dept. of Public Instruction
Old Capitol Building
Washington & Legion
Mail Stop FG-11
Olympia, WA 98504

West Virginia

State Superintendent of Schools
State Dept. of Education
1900 Washington Street
Building 6, Room 358
Charleston, WV 25305

Wisconsin

Superintendent of Public
   Instruction
State Dept. of Public Instruction
125 South Webster Street
P.O. Box 7841
Madison, WI 53707

Wyoming

State Superintendent of Public
   Instruction
State Dept. of Education
Hathaway Building
Cheyenne, WY 82002

*Council of Chief State School
   Officers*

Executive Director
Council of Chief State School
   Officers
379 Hall of the States
400 North Capitol Street NW
Washington, DC 20001

Appendix I

Journals in Gifted Education

G/C/T
350 Weinacker Avenue
Mobile, AL 36604

This magazine serves as a resource to parents, teachers, and other professionals interested in gifted and creative youth. It is published five times per year.

Gifted Child Quarterly
1155 15th Street NW #1002
Washington, DC 20005

The journal focuses on research, program description and evaluation, and other topics of interest in the field of gifted education. It is published by the National Association for Gifted Children.

Journal of Creative Behavior
Creative Educational Foundations, Inc.
State University College
1300 Elmwood Avenue
Buffalo, NY 14222

The focus of the journal is primarily research and program practices in the area of creative behavior in children and adults.

Journal for the Education of the Gifted
1920 Association Drive
Reston, VA 22091

Articles on programs, research, and other related topics in gifted education appear in this publication. It is the official journal of The Association for the Gifted.

Roeper Review
Roeper City and County Schools
2190 North Woodward
Bloomfield Hills, MI 48013

Theme issues are frequently published in this journal. Although research articles are published along with program descriptions, practical applications are given.

INDEX